Dec 66 - N. M. 4.66

367

MARIONETTES

MARIONETTES

Easy to Make!   *Fun to Use!*

By EDITH FLACK ACKLEY

**With forty-one black and white drawings by
MARJORIE FLACK**

J. B. LIPPINCOTT COMPANY

PHILADELPHIA   **NEW YORK**

Library of Congress catalog card number 29-18474

PRINTED IN THE UNITED STATES OF AMERICA

CONTENTS

INTRODUCTION

THIS little book seems to me like a bright stone cast into the Pool of Happiness. I can hear the splash of laughter which will greet it and see the widening ripples of smiles as each new possessor rejoices in its spell.

Having known and loved Edith Flack Ackley's Little People for years, I am convinced that everyone, children and so-called Grown-ups alike, need marionettes—children, because they live so near the Never-never Land of Whimsical Make-believe that these tiny actors seem real playmates; older children—called Men and Women—because, having danced so long as Fate has pulled the strings, there is fascination in the making and manipulation of these light-hearted puppets so responsive to every mood save that of sadness.

For some reason we have been denied our heritage of friendship with marionettes in this country. The few we have heretofore met with have been elaborate dolls with something of the commonplace qualities of real life.

But these marionettes eager to pirouette into your home from between the covers of this book, are beings from a world all their own of sunshine devoid of shadow, gay, somewhat fantastic, altogether charming.

A few bits of cloth and scraps of silk or cotton; a snip or two of the scissors and some stitches with needle and thread—out of these materials within the reach of every hand Edith Flack Ackley has created a new joy for the busy fingers of Childhood and for those grown weary from the sober work of Life.

L. WALKER ERSKINE.

MARIONETTES

Chapter I

MARIONETTES—THEIR UNIVERSAL CHARM

IT is a great joy to know before you start, that your audience is going to like your work. You can be sure that young and old, unsophisticated and conventional people, everyone, everywhere, will like puppets.

The appeal, the magnetism of puppets is not to be explained in everyday words; but it is true that their magical charm strikes a responsive, sympathetic chord in every heart.

To manipulate a marionette yourself, to bring life to a little inanimate body gives you a breathless joy, a mysterious sense of power.

Puppets—for the word "puppet" covers all types of figures, and "marionette" applies to those manipulated by

1

strings or wires—have a history that begins with the first efforts of people to make images of gods and men, for worship or entertainment.

In Europe and Asia there has evidently been this love for puppets since the beginning of civilization.

Puppets are woven through the ancient history of Egypt and the Orient. They are found in the pagan and religious rites of Greece and Rome. They appear in the writings of Plato and Apuleius.

The famous Pulcinella, a buffoon, was probably created by a Neapolitan about 1600. Pulcinella's descendants have traveled far since then. In England there is Mr. Punch; in Germany—Pulzinella; and in France—Polichinelle or Guignol.

In France the first permanent marionette stage was built about 1649, although puppets had visited the country from Italy as early as 1630. They grew in popularity until not only were they a familiar sight in public places, but were also found in the castles and homes of the cultured poeple.

They spread rapidly through Germany and England and some of the greatest writers and musicians in these and other countries became interested in them. Goethe, Goldoni the great Italian dramatist, and Voltaire had their own puppet stages and wrote puppet plays. Haydn composed marionette operas; Gounod wrote the "Funeral March of a Marionette"; George Sand and her son Maurice with their clever puppets and plays gave pleasure to their friends.

Today, although Germany, England, and Russia have interesting puppets, the French are unquestionably the most ingenious with their puppet shows. Anyone in Paris can easily find the type of Guignol performance he fancies—in the Luxembourg Gardens, on the Champs Élysée, or in the real theatres devoted to marionettes.

In Spain and Sicily you can still find the old type of marionette, four or five feet high, clad in heavy armor, carrying on from night to night the tales of Charlemagne.

In Vienna today Richard Teschner has fashioned a tiny stage as beautiful as a shrine and for it has carved exquisite little figures of linden wood. His pantomimes of fairy-tales and myths carry the fortunate beholder into a fanciful world of unreality.

Puppets have been made of various materials, in many styles and sizes. The oldest were of terra-cotta. Other ancient ones were of bone, ivory and carved wood. Some were of wax and wood, and others of wood and cloth. Perhaps the most interesting of all were the old shadow puppets of the Orient, made of carefully stretched hide, beautifully gilded, colored and pierced. These were manipulated by slender rods of bamboo or horn, and so placed between a light and screen that the colored shadows appeared to the audience. You can still see shadow plays in China, India and Java.

Here in America we know very little about puppets, although our Indians did have articulated figures for their corn festivals and ceremonial dances.

In this country at present we have about fifteen or twenty professionals giving puppet entertainments in different parts of the United States, but almost every one of them is making the conventional, traditional foreign type of puppet, constructing the heads of modeled papier-mâché or carved wood. This book tells how to make them very easily from cloth.

The first taste of puppet art has awakened an interest that is rapidly becoming country-wide. There is a vast audience eager and ready for marionettes, and there is no reason why there should not be new, originally designed marionettes sponsored by our own artists, writers and musicians.

Think how delightful it would be to have small theatres devoted to marionettes, where different companies could play! Think of the exquisite spectacles that could be produced by artists and poets! Think of the humorous, clever parodies of the stage that could be given by marionettes! And think of the delightful, naïve productions of marionettes manipulated by the hands of children. Big theatres, little theatres, movie theatres we have—but to round out the theatrical cycle of today we need the marionette theatres with their irresistible little actors.

We need marionettes in our homes and in the schools. They are fun! Everything connected with marionettes is not only joyful but of immense value in the development of dramatic talent. It is splendid training in color, speech and rhythm. In the creating and staging of such plays there is opportunity for experience in making costumes, scenery and furniture.

Marionettes themselves do not necessarily have to be complicated affairs. Do not be afraid to make the first one.

The simplest clown, even though crudely made, at the moment it is given the power to move, is given also the power to capture the imagination and affection of the beholder!

This book is written hoping that you will find it a practical help in constructing marionettes which are simple, capable, and of pleasant appearance. A marionette, to be successful artistically, should be simple in construction, having as little exaggerated action as possible; yet capable of showing all necessary emotions. Most certainly it should be of pleasing appearance.

You will find that marionettes made from patterns found in the pocket at the back of the book, are adequate foundation for professional entertainments, and yet simple enough for children to make in school or camp.

There should be marionette performances in every city, town and village: and I hope the children of this generation will put them there, for the enjoyment and enchantment of all children and grown-ups.

Chapter II

MAKING MARIONETTES

MATERIALS.—The materials needed for the marionette bodies are: cotton crêpe or fine muslin, hospital cotton for stuffing, and lead of some sort for weight in feet, hands and seat. Solder, shot, or sinkers can be used. In a large hardware store it is possible to buy solder in the form of a flat wire about an eighth of an inch wide—but do not buy the kind that has an acid core. This is ideal to use because it can easily be folded and can be cut with scissors. If you cannot buy the solder, get shot or two sizes of lead sinkers such as are made for fishing. A tiny size about one-half an inch long is used for hands and feet, and a size that is about two inches long to weight the seats of the marionettes.

The Japanese crêpe of pale yellow is the most satisfactory, as the color is fresh and clean in the footlights and the crêpe forces into the desired shape more easily than muslin. Pink is apt to look greyish. White can be used or white can be dipped in pale yellow tintex or similar dye.

Clean white hospital cotton packs best and doesn't fly and tickle the inside of your nose while you work.

Cutting.—When you use the patterns in the back pocket of the book, do not cut them but make tracings on thin paper and cut the tracings. This will keep your original patterns intact so that they can be used over and over again.

It is a good idea to begin with a clown so that your first attempt at marionette-making will be a sure success. On page 62 you will find suggestions for entertaining with one clown.

Using the pattern marked "Adult," make tracing of body, legs, arms and head. Cut out these tracings. Have the crêpe folded lengthwise (selvage parallel with selvage); lay one of your cut-out tracings lengthwise on it. Baste or pin it securely and draw around it with a pencil, but do not cut your material. As you remove your tracing put two or three pins in the crêpe to keep the two pieces from slipping.

Sewing.—Sew by hand with a double thread, or by sewing machine, just on the pencil line, leaving the openings as indicated on the pattern. If you go outside the line the pencil mark will show when the piece is turned right side out.

It is wise to take back stitches around the wrists and ankles, and overcasting the seam when cut adds strength.

Now cut your goods not more than a quarter of an inch from the sewing and turn each piece right side out. A bone or wooden knitting needle is a help when turning arms and legs.

Stuffing.—For the weights in each foot use a piece of solder about two inches long folded, or a small sinker. Wrap a film of cotton around it and slip it into the foot. Proceed to stuff it with small wads of cotton, using a pencil or knitting needle to push it down through the leg. Do not pack the foot very full but legs may be packed firm and hard.

When the foot is stuffed turn it up to look like a foot and sew it in that position; then go on stuffing until the pattern shows you where to sew across for the knee. A ballet dancer's foot can be left straight down and packed hard.

Stuff the arms firmly, putting small pieces of solder, or a tiny sinker, in the hands and sewing at the elbow as indicated in the pattern.

The torso can be stuffed full for an ordinary marionette and left hollow in the center for a more pliable figure such as an Oriental dancer would need. If the center is left hollow, hold your cotton in place at top and bottom by stitches through the crepe.

When the torso is sewed up, you can attach the arms; gather the tops and sew them on with strong stitches. Try the arms to see that they can be raised straight up in the air.

The legs are not gathered. The raw edges can be turned in and overcast with double thread to the torso. An unstuffed space of an inch at the top of the leg allows more freedom of movement.

The head should be stuffed as tightly as possible. Press the cotton down hard with your fingers, fold the top down neatly like a box and sew it. See that no corners stick up to poke through the hair.

By experimenting with small pieces of folded crêpe, ears and noses can be evolved for grotesque or comic characters. Giants, witches and clowns often benefit by having ears and protruding noses, but unless made and applied with extreme care such features are too conspicuous for most marionettes.

Next seam the top and side of the neck; turn the piece, but do not stuff it, and overcast it at the top to the head, just back of the chin seam.

If you will finish the head before you fasten the lower part of the neck to the shoulders you will find it easier to handle.

Hair.—The hair is successfully and easily made of Columbia Floss or similar wool.

You will find that you can lift whole sections of wool off the ball. Cut across the strands and without losing any of the threads, arrange on the head. Lay a section of wool over the top of the head to form long bangs over the face. If they are short you have no chance to rearrange, so make them quite long. Hold it in place and sew with occasional back stitches across the top of the head. Sew with thread, not wool, and have the color to match or at least be near enough in color to be inconspicuous. A good foundation arrangement is made in this fashion.

Now cut another section and place it crosswise on the head having the sides even, then sew it on the top of the

"JESTER"   "MOTHER"   "SUSIE"   "SANTA"

head at each side to hold the strands in place. You may cut the back and sides but leave the front long until you decide on the final arrangement of the short bangs or parted effect.

Embroidery silk makes beautiful braids for Princesses and black velvet makes very sleek hair. Sections of wool an inch long sewed through the middle and each section pushed close up against the other forms a head of hair that can be cut in a variety of ways. When the hair is arranged, sew the features.

Features.—If you cut papers the size of your marionette's face, you can try out with a pencil different effects in expression—there are suggestions illustrated. Keep the expression simple. You will be surprised to find that there is an illusion of changing expression when the marionette appears behind the footlights. An exaggerated expression becomes tiring and creates no illusion; leave something to the imagination of your audience.

You can draw lightly on your material with pencil, but it is best of all to try directly with your needle for it can be

"HAPPY"   "JANE"   "BLACKBOY"   "OLGA"

easily changed—that is one of the many advantages of thread over paint.

For the outline of the eyes and eyebrows use two strands of black mercerized darning cotton and sew with a regular outline stitch. You may make the iris of blue embroidery floss if you like, but black darning cotton gives a lasting, clear black outline that carries well to the last row in the audience.

Use red sewing silk for the mouth, filling in with solid stitches where necessary. Put in two silk stitches for the nostrils. Then for a finishing touch use a red pencil on the cheeks to give a healthy look to such marionettes as need it. Experiment on a piece of crêpe first.

Neck.—Now hold the lower part of the neck onto the torso to determine the correct length, have it long enough so that the head can fall forward on the chest. Sew it firmly to the body at the seam but do not bother to turn in the raw edges, for the clothes cover any left-over material hanging down the back. Go back and forth several times with your stitches and use a double thread too—I have seen heads come off at critical times!

Now cut a piece of solder about six inches long and fold it into a piece the width of the back of your marionette's body. A large sinker will do as well as the solder. Cover it with a piece of crêpe and sew it to the bottom of the back. Try making the marionette sit on the edge of the table. This weight keeps him from sliding off too easily and makes him more willing to sit down in the first place.

Then your marionette is ready to dress, and the next chapter will tell you how to do it.

Animals.—Animals can be made of rough cloth, thin flexible leather, velvet, plush or real fur if it has a close nap.

Make a pattern the general shape of the animal you desire. Look at the animal patterns in the pocket at the back of the book to see the construction. You will find that after the animal is sewed and stuffed, alterations can be made on the outside to help the expression. Find a picture of the animal you are making and by using correct ears, whiskers, tail, etc., you can portray the animal so that it is easily recognized—a little exaggeration sometimes helps.

The neck of the animal should not be stuffed. If the animal is small, a cat or dog for instance, do not stuff the body. Stuff only the head and weight the feet.

Large animals can have their bodies held out by a cardboard box—a little cotton will pad the corners.

Donkeys or horses can have legs made separate from the body and stiffened by sticks inside the cloth. Sew the legs

HOBBY HORSE

to the body with very loose stitches and wind thread around the stitches as you do when sewing on a button, or attach them by a wire run through the body.

The leg should be able to swing freely back and forth. Large animals can have circles of leather for the soles of their feet.

Expressive eyes can be made of shoe buttons, with bits of white leather behind them. Beads or fancy buttons make beautiful eyes, green ones, yellow ones, blue ones!

Tails and manes can be made of fringed leather, cloth, wool floss or unraveled rope. Tails should be given special attention and always have their own string attached.

A clever horse can be made with nothing more than a little rustic table to which is added a rope tail and cardboard head! The clowns can be very funny with him if one holds onto the tail of the horse while the other clown rides. Hobby horses of cardboard and a stick are funny too.

And Snakes.—Snakes slither across a stage in a manner most terrifying! Metallic silk material makes very snaky snakes. You will have no trouble making one if you use a pointed tube-like shape, cutting your goods on the bias instead of on the straight of the goods. Insert a small piece of card-board to hold the head flat, and two bead eyes and a forked tongue.

In the body insert, at intervals of an inch or two, small folded pieces of solder wrapped in crêpe. Stitch through the skin of the snake to hold the weights in place; a bit of fluffed up cotton can be used in the body in one or two places if the snake is large and fearsome.

Chapter III

COSTUMING

COSTUMING marionettes is important. Take time to have the right type for the character because clothes express even more for marionettes than they do for people.

Color.—Color is the first thing to consider after the style is planned. The easiest way is to place your figure on the stage and try pinning materials on it. If you have a spotlight with color screens, try out the effect of different screens on the hair and materials. Children care a great deal about the colors of the clothes of their favorites and they usually prefer blond silken braids for the heroines and black hair for their heroes!

Materials.—Avoid stiff, heavy materials as far as possible. They hinder action and do not drape well on such small people. Velvet, satin, soft silks and chiffons are suitable—wash materials should be soft and fresh looking. Solid colors are usually more effective than patterns unless the patterns are in proportion to the size of the marionette. Always have your materials as beautiful as possible; dowdy clothes take away so much from the fineness of a production. The children who come back stage should find the Princess just as royal as they thought her, or even more so. Of course you cannot express poverty without rags but the rags can at least be of soft inconspicuous material.

Sewing.—The sewing part need not be tedious. You are not dressmaking—you are making a picture with fabrics, taking stitches only where absolutely necessary. Too much sewing often ruins the effect. Do not hem any part that you can leave unhemmed. By cutting the material by a drawn thread you can have a tiny fringed edge which is better than a hem that is so apt to be stiff and awkward. If you are afraid to cut directly into your material (but try not to be), cut pieces of paper or old cloth to try the size.

Marionettes cannot have their clothes changed because of the strings; therefore you can sew each piece firmly to the marionette as you go along. Do not sew the sleeves into the armholes as a dressmaker does; it is not necessary to sew the shoulder seams before the waist is on unless you are very clever at dressmaking, and even so I shouldn't risk it.

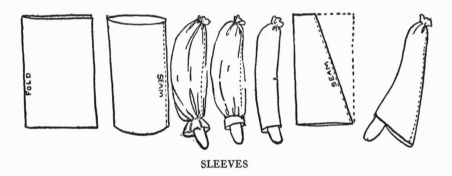

SLEEVES

Sleeves—Warning.—The elbow *must* have room to bend *freely!* Do not have the sleeve too tight from the top of the arm to the wrist—have it so loose that the forearm can bend straight back onto the upper arm. You can see by the illustration how a perfectly straight piece can be made into a sleeve—full for a girl or snug (not forgetting the important elbow) for a man.

A folded piece of goods may be wrapped tightly over the ruffle and fastened in place if you would rather have a cuff effect at the wrist.

By seaming diagonally and cutting off the triangles you can have a decorative type of sleeve—see the illustration.

The top of any sleeve will be covered by the waist so do not turn in the top when you gather it.

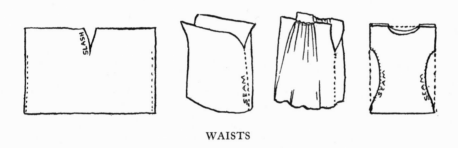

WAISTS

Waists.—A simple bodice or waist can be made in one piece. Measure your marionette for length and width; then sew the seam up as far as the under arm, leaving enough material for turning raw edges under on the shoulder. Make a slash in the goods on the other side to equal the opening you have left on the first side.

Put this on the figure and fold under the raw edges around the arms, taking a stitch or two to hold it in place. Lap the front slightly over the back on the shoulders for about one-half an inch or so, turn the front under a little to hide raw edges, sew this to the shoulder, then gather the neck if you have made a full waist.

If you wish a snug fit you can cut your waist in two pieces (back and front) instead of one, and curve them a little on the sides.

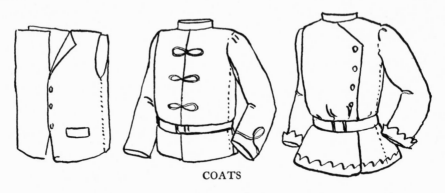

COATS

Coats.—A coat effect can be easily made by cutting straight down the center front and turning back the upper corners for lapels—arranging the shoulder seams in the same way as the waist.

A shirt and collar can be suggested by a piece of white linen handkerchief. Do not forget the necktie of some pliable material or ribbon.

A high coat collar can be made of a straight folded piece of goods arranged about the neck and sewed to the coat.

Bits of fur, lace and gold braid, used judiciously, add glamour to a costume.

SKIRTS

Skirts.—Skirts and petticoats are made of straight strips of material. Measure the marionette from the waist down to determine the length of the skirt. Have the skirt fuller and longer than the petticoat, for if you don't the petticoat will hang badly and show below the skirt.

Sew the seam, place it at the back, (the marionette being now inside the skirt) and sew it to the figure. Now take stitches through the gathers to hold the skirt securely in place so that there will be no sagging or ripping. Ruffles, borders, sashes and aprons are effective.

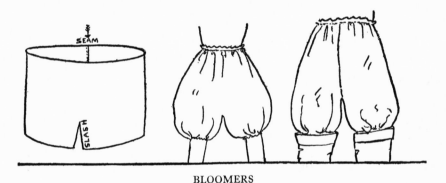

BLOOMERS

Bloomers.—Bloomers can be made by making a slash in a petticoat and sewing seams to form legs, then gathering the waist and the bottoms of the legs.

Hats and Head-dresses.—Hats and head-dresses often are a help in expressing the character of a marionette. Avoid large stiff hats as they are apt to prove troublesome and interfere with the head strings and the shoulder strings when the head tips back and forth.

A turban is easily made by winding a strip of silk about the head; scarfs are colorful for gypsies; a Dutch cap is

"WILFRED"   "DWARF"   "SANTA"   "BLACKBOY"

pretty and not hard to arrange with a handkerchief. A tam-o-shanter can be made by cutting two circles, the same size, out of your material. A bread and butter plate and a piece of chalk will help you. Baste the two pieces together wrong side out, and make a tiny seam. Next cut in the center of one side a circular opening smaller than the head size of the marionette; then try it on and cut the hole to the exact size. Turn the tam right side out and tack it in place on the head, turning the raw edge under.

Footwear.—To make a shoe, cut an oval a little larger than the bottom of the foot for the sole, then cut a top similar to the shoe pattern in pocket at the back of the book. Place the two pieces with the toes together, the leather right side out, as your sewing is to be done on the right side. Use a medium-sized needle—one that will carry number 50 cotton, as this is the easiest size to push through leather. With an over-and-over stitch sew from the center of the toe around to the heel, then start at the center of the toe again and sew the other side. You will probably find leather left over at the back—cut this off and overcast the seam. Straps and buckles, rosettes and bows can be added.

"JESTER"   "SUSIE"   "JIMMIE"   "PERCY"

To make a boot, use the shoe pattern for the lower part and for the leg make a tube of leather to fit inside the top of the shoe. Sew the leg part on the marionette before you attach the shoe part. Have all footwear firmly sewed to the figure.

In the pocket at the back of the book you will find a pattern for a clown's costume. It can be made of solid color with contrasting ruffles and circles or pompons—or of half black and half white—the black sleeve being on the white side of the body.

If you will make your first marionette a clown you can feel certain that your first attempt will be a success. Special dancers are fascinating, but music must be tried out and to perfect their performances, practice in control is required. A jerked arm or leg at the wrong time is most ruinous. Ludicrous accidents can happen most unexpectedly if you are not well acquainted with your temperamental dancers.

But a clown—that is a different matter! He becomes at once a faithful friend. He is funny, he is willing; in fact, he does half the job himself. He does not even require a

stage or music but is amazingly droll, climbing into laps
and falling out again, staggering about the room, tripping
over his own feet or sitting on the floor doing nothing at all
but gazing into space with inscrutable eyes. All his antics
are funny in spite of you and you may trust him to be
irresistible.

Chapter IV

STRINGING AND MANIPULATING

T HE hard work is now behind you and if you have taken my advice, you have a nice limp clown all dressed, ready to string up to the control. If you haven't a clown, it is probably a Dutch girl or an Oriental dancer, and you may have to be a little more patient.

You will like putting the strings on the marionette and adjusting them and making them fast to the control—but if it happens that you don't like making the control itself, have a carpenter make some for you.

Here is what you will need for an ordinary control and the way to make it. The width of the wood is not as important as the length. Soft wood is best but I have used drift wood and even stolen the wood out of window shades.

Now look at the drawing:

No. I is a strip 11 inches long and 1¼ inches wide.

No. II is a strip 4½ inches long and ½ inch wide. It is nailed with small wire nails on to No. I at one end.

No. III is a strip 8½ inches long and ½ inch wide. It is nailed on to No. 1 behind No. II. The distance between No. II and No. III is 1¼ inches.

No. IV is a strip 10 inches long and ½ inch wide. This is not nailed to anything; it is held in the right hand, while the main control is in your left. (I'll tell you

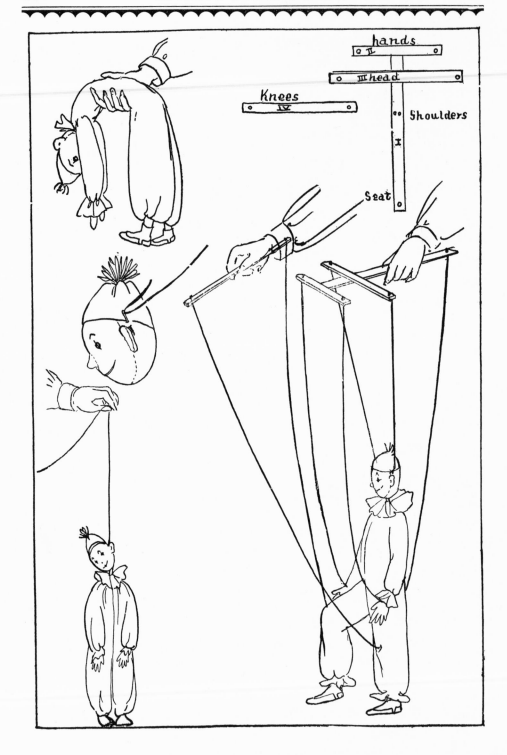

this now in case you are curious and I hope you *are* curious.)

After your nailing is done (or before, it doesn't matter when) drill holes in the ends of No. II, No. III, and No. IV and at the back of No. I, also two holes near edges of No. 1, six inches from the front. Use an ordinary hand drill. If you like a well-done job, sandpaper the edges a little.

For stringing regular marionettes, I use Aunt Lydia's carpet thread, but I like still better a fine fish-line called Cuttyhunk No. VI. It is strong and doesn't snarl and knot. For fairies and other small creatures, I use heavy black linen thread. Thread your string through a pointed Crewel needle or darning-needle but do not cut the string. Take your defenseless clown, or whoever it is you have created, stick the needle (pointing downward) through his skin just behind and above his ear, or where he would naturally have an ear. (See the drawing.) Pull your string through the cloth—just the one stitch—slip the string out of the needle and tie a knot in the end of the string. You are still fastened to the spool. Give the string a yank and you will know whether you have made the knot large enough or not. If it is too low or too far forward, his head will have a tendency to fall backward when the strings are relaxed.

Now stand up, hold your arms straight out as high as is comfortable for you—your hands slightly higher than your waistline. For the average marionette the head string measures 30 inches to the control. Dangle your marionette at the end of the string with his feet on the floor and cut your string, allowing about six inches above your hand, these six inches are allowed for tying and altering.

Now sit down comfortably and put the string back of the other ear. Measure and cut this string by the first one. Fasten strings the same way on the marionette's back at the shoulders and bottom. (See the drawing.) Remember when you measure the back strings to have the marionette straight upright. The same way when you measure for the hands—have them straight down at the sides. Put the needle directly through the hand, from back to palm; leave it sticking in while you lift the string to find out if the arm lifts naturally. If it doesn't, try the needle in another place, perhaps more on top of the hand. When it seems right, then tie your knot.

The knee strings go from the front to the back, knotted under the knee. Lay the marionette on the floor if it is easier to measure the strings.

You may need someone to help you tie the strings to the control. I use my teeth. If you don't tie your knots tightly they are easier to adjust.

A. Tie your head strings first to the ends of No. III; look down at your marionette and see that he stands with his feet on the floor, knees stiff.

B. Tie the shoulder strings through the two holes near the center of No. I, holding the control horizontally.

C. Tie the lower back string through the hole at the back of No. I, being sure you hold the control level, or having someone hold it for you. When you tie these three back strings, don't tie them so tight that the weight of the marionette is taken off the head strings.

D. Tie the hands strings through the holes of No. II—if you haven't made the usual mistake of tying the head strings on it. Have the hands straight down at the sides. Have the strings neither taut nor loose. A tape or strap can be tacked across the top of this stick (No. II) to form a loop to put your hand through when you wish to hold a marionette in each hand.

Now try your marionette. Hold the control in your left hand and with your right forefinger hooked lift the arm string. Don't reach far down the string—lift near the control. Learn this the first whack out-of-the-box and your hands won't be seen on the stage. "Oh, I see a hand!" from the audience, isn't pleasant. Try hooking one of your left fingers under the shoulder strings, pressing it back an inch or so against the bottom of the control. This lets the head fall forward. Try tipping the control forward and back, keeping the shoulder strings under the finger. Try tipping the control left to right and notice what it does to the head.

E. Tie up the knee strings through the holes in the single stick (No. IV). Have them long enough so that when you lay this stick between No. II and No. III the knees aren't lifted. See that the legs hang perfectly straight.

Now with the control in your left hand, the leg stick in your right, with good quick music on the radio or phonograph or sung by yourself, start tilting the leg stick up and down—hold your right hand a foot or so from your left—and walk around the room. Try hooking your right forefinger around an arm string without letting go the leg stick; try making him climb up on a chair; get his arms up on the seat first then raise one knee—and so on. He ought to be a very willing and happy clown and you a proud parent.

If there is any trouble, read the directions all over again and look at the drawings to see that you have made no mistake. Then if there is still trouble, try shifting the knee strings to the right or left. Cut off the knot under the knee, pull out the string, rethread your needle, put it in a better place and make a new knot. To make a good kick I sometimes put the thread through the top of the lower leg, instead of through the bottom of the upper leg. This stringing is a good foundation for all marionettes. You can add strings, if desirable—see the drawing.

To make the clown stand on his hands put strings on his

heels and tie these strings to a second leg stick. To make it easier to hold, drive a nail through No. I just back of No. II to hold the regular leg stick and another just in front of the hole at the other end of No. I for the heel stick, having made a hole in the center of each leg stick so it can be slipped over the nail when not in use. For extra long funny feet use toe strings as well as knee strings. To make the hands come to the hips, (see the Gypsy drawing), sew small metal rings on her hips. Put an extra string on the tip of each hand, run it through each ring and up above the control. Let the hands hang straight down; tie your strings together and keep a thumb-tack on No. I just in front of the shoulder strings to slip it under when not in use. When you lift on the loop her hands will fly to her hips; lift her regular hand strings and they fly out again.

To make a clown juggle a ball, drill a smooth hole through a wooden ball, run both regular hand strings through it, but instead of fastening them to the regular stick, tie them to a separate one about twelve inches long. It sounds too simple, but he will really throw the ball from one hand to the other and up in the air as you tip the stick. If the clown has kid hands put strings through them so that palms are up.

Characters in plays who have long skirts can attain a very natural walk without knee strings. In moving them across the stage, break the walk by having them turn a little and pause, speak and raise a hand occasionally.

For animals make a control about the length of your animal. (They usually have just the one control.) In stringing up a donkey have the main control (stick No. I, which is 1¼ inches wide) the length of your animal. Mine is thirteen inches long. Nail one cross piece ten inches long an inch from the end. Drill holes each end of the cross piece. Drill two holes at the front corners of No. I, two more at edges 2½ inches back, two more the same distance from the back end and then one in the middle of the back end. Tie his ears to the first pair of holes; tie the head strings through the holes in the cross piece, the shoulders

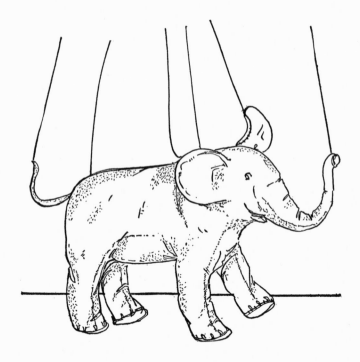

through the second pair of holes, his rear strings near the tail through the third pair of holes and his tail through the single middle hole at the end. He ought to be very lively and I think you'll find him so when he winks an ear.

An elephant needs a little stick, about four inches long,

nailed out in front of the main control for his trunk string.

If the animal has a very long tail, like a lion, nail a small stick on the back end of stick No. I—the same idea as for the elephant trunk.

If this isn't all you need in the way of information on stringing you can get a great deal more by experimenting.

If the strings tangle, get someone to hold the controls, take hold of the back string where it is attached to the marionette and by following it up to the control you can easily see which way the stick has been turned over.

When manipulating the marionettes, it is usual to hold the large control in the left hand and the leg stick in the right. Remember that pressing the shoulder strings up against the underside of the control lets the head fall forward. Your right hand fingers must become agile enough to pick up hand strings and not drop the leg stick.

At first you and the marionette will be awkward unless you are very remarkable. You will look at your hands and the strings and wonder which string does what. But very soon you will be able to make the marionette obey you and his short freedom will be over.

Manipulation soon becomes second nature to you; you must practice until you have perfect control and then you will be surprised to find yourself entirely forgetting the strings.

The dancers are particularly fascinating to control. Your first instinct may be to keep time to the music with your own feet but after you become familiar with the

"AT FIRST YOU AND THE MARIONETTE WILL BE AWKWARD."

balance of a dancer and you have listened carefully several times to the music you will find that your feeling of the rhythm carries through the strings to your marionette without conscious effort on your part.

Chapter V

STAGES

THE simplest way to improvise a stage is to use an arch-way. If there are draperies at each side, draw them enough to leave an opening three feet wide; block out the center by hanging on the pole another curtain or piece of material to reach within twenty-five inches of the floor. Pin the sides of the center curtain to the draperies.

A card table stood on edge forms a practical background to hide you, or a rope or rod can be arranged to support a curtain. Have your background several inches higher than the opening of the stage, and placed about a foot and a half back of it.

If you must use an ordinary doorway, block out the top of the opening so that a proscenium arch is formed twenty-five inches high and the width of your doorway. Arrange a protection for yourself about a foot and a half back of this.

When you cannot use a doorway of any kind you can resort to sheets to form your curtains; hang them from a rope or rod just a little higher than your head.

With these improvised stages, where you use the floor for your stage boards, your audience should sit on the same level.

Small Portable Stage.—The small portable stage shown in the drawing is a practical and satisfactory stage for all ordinary entertainments. It is easy to construct, the materials are not expensive.

This efficient portable stage, light in weight and com-

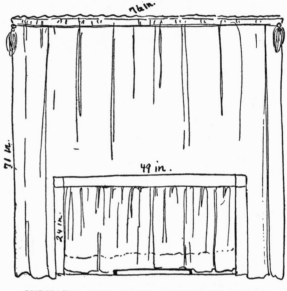

CURTAINS FOR SMALL PORTABLE STAGE

pact enough to carry by taxi and train, is a necessity if you are going to give many entertainments. The portable stage shown in the drawing is small enough to set up in a living room and is large enough to use in a club house, Parish house, school or hall. It seems like magic to have such a large stage come out of such a small case. The backgrounds and some marionettes can be packed with the stage and usually one suitcase will carry everything else that you need—marionettes, phonograph records, thumbtacks, etc.

The background screen is made of four sections of
beaver board—the hinges are of brass put on with split
rivets. Small sockets bent up out of brass hold the side rods.

The rods are commonly known as "dowel rods" and may
be purchased at any lumber supply house. Select straight

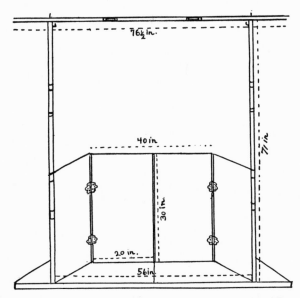

FRAMEWORK OF SMALL PORTABLE STAGE

ones, seven half-inch ones for sides and top and three
slightly smaller for the drop curtain. Fishing-rod ferrules
should be used for the joints. Headless nails should be
inserted in the top of each upper side rod to fit in holes
drilled in the top rods. See the drawing for the measure-
ments.

The rods of the drop curtain, when fitted together,
should be long enough to rest on the screen when down.
When raised it can rest on two nails driven into the upper
side rods near the top of the main curtain.

The little footlight reflector is the right length for three little, clear glass, 25 watt, showcase bulbs wired in a row. The reflector itself can be made of aluminum or tin.

A spotlight can be made to fasten on the background screen if you like. Little one-bulb reflectors can be bought at electrical stores.

Curtains.—The curtains of marionette stages to conceal the manipulations should be of light weight curtain material; silk is by far the most beautiful and satisfactory. Velvet absorbs a surprising amount of sound and adds too much weight to your outfit. Drapery departments of the stores carry a variety of suitable materials and colors.

The colors of your curtains should be so chosen that they will harmonize with any surroundings—gold, soft blues or greens are good. My own curtains for both large and small portable stages are made of a shimmering blue silk and the drop curtains are of a lighter blue shot through with silver. I have elaborate green velvet curtains, gorgeous with gold and ornamented with brilliant appliqués, but I seldom use them because they deaden sound and are so heavy. I also have a set for a nursery stage. They are made of yellow and orange cotton crêpe, cheerfully embroidered with colored wool flowers.

If the material of your curtains is so thin that your audience can see your outlines, hang a piece of black paper muslin back of the center part.

The floor is the best place for your cutting and basting. After the basting is done on your large curtain and the top hem sewed in try it on your rod to see if it hangs as it should.

Have the drop curtain touch the floor so that marionette feet will not show before the curtain goes up.

A fiber case the size of your background screen and about four inches thick, is not expensive to have made. It will carry your screen, rods, back-drops and some of the marionettes. An inexpensive case for the screen and rods can be made of canvas. Make it like a large envelope— with a flap.

When you arrange for your show you usually ask, "Have you a table five feet long strong enough to stand on?" and if they haven't one—"Have you a small steady table and two card tables?" The card tables can be used to support the stage while you and your assistant stand on the strong table in back. Usually schools, club rooms and Parish houses have large tables that will hold you, your assistant and the stage.

When giving the entertainment for children in a private home the stage can be set up on the floor instead of on the tables, though of course it is not as effective and the children have to sit on the floor to see.

Remember to ask if they have a phonograph. If you are giving many performances (and each one you do will usually bring you three more engagements) you will need a portable phonograph of your own.

By using tables you do not have to carry a heavy supporting structure. All other marionette stages that I have seen have to be carried in a truck. It also makes it easier to set the stage up in a hurry; thirty minutes after the time

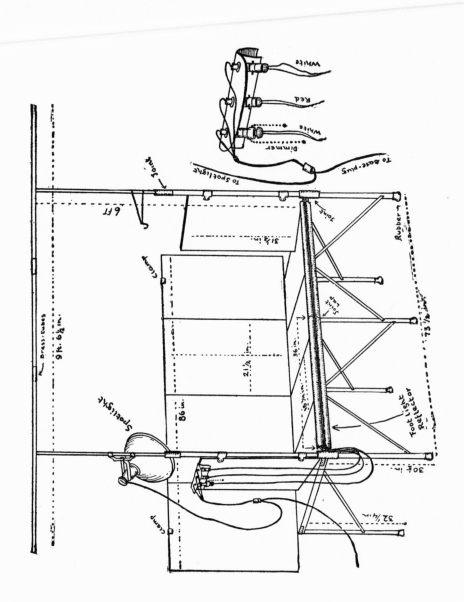

you enter the room with your baggage should find the stage up and everything ready for the word to begin the show.

Large Portable Stage.—It is possible to construct a large portable stage in exactly the same way as the small—increasing the length of the stage opening, the background, drop curtain, etc.

If you wish a more elaborate large stage the drawing given here will help you to make one or furnish an idea for a carpenter.

This stage is designed so that it can be taken apart and packed in a steamer trunk. The framework is very light, the greater part of it being made of dowel rods. The legs are braced by aluminum rods bent at the end to hook into holes in the wooden strips that hold the floor. The floor of the platform is four sections of beaver board that rest on a rabbet. The background is a four-section beaver board screen and the two wings are of beaver board. Brass hinges are used for the background; two tubes of brass on each wing slip over the bottom side rods.

The stage floor is ordinary table height so that you can use any steady table to stand on when you give the performance. The footlight reflector of aluminum hooks onto the front of the stage. The outside of this should be painted black. The floodlight, which is a regular store-window floodlight made to use colored screens, is clamped onto the front upright above the right wing. The control for the footlights is hung on the outside of this wing. There are ten footlights—25 watt, clear glass, tubular bulbs. Four are wired to one control, three to another and three red

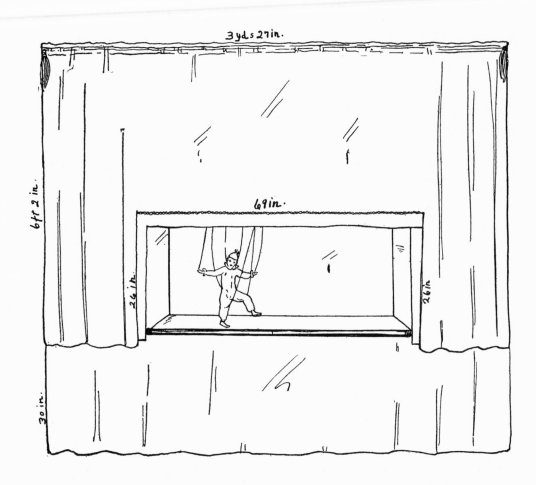

ones to the third. These three red ones are at intervals across the front. The bank of three white ones can be green if you wish more variety of color effects.

The curtains for this stage are made on the same principle as the small stage curtains, and a piece of black material, such as black sateen, is carried to cover the lower framework of the stage.

Nails should be driven in the upper side rods to rest the drop curtain on when it is raised. When it is down it will rest on the wings.

On the small stage the marionettes must enter between the curtain and the edge of the screen but on this stage you can have regular exits of course.

Chapter VI

STAGE SETTINGS

THE back-drop or background of the stage is a very important part of the production. It can make the atmosphere of the act successful or, if not in keeping with the marionettes appearing in the scene, ruin the entire effect.

I have worked out backgrounds suitable for my marionettes, that are easy to make, that pack well without mussing, and can be quickly changed during the performance.

The beaver board, whether for large or small portable stage (as described in Chapter V), should be covered with gold paper. The Japan Paper Company of New York carries a number of styles and patterns that are very beautiful. Put your glue on the screen (not on the paper), in strips forming a four-inch crossbar pattern; then lay your dry paper on it. This keeps the screen from pulling out of shape.

It is comparatively easy to decide on the scenery for interiors and outdoor sets, though you must remember to keep them subdued in tone and secondary to your characters; in other words, keep your back-drop truly a background for the action of the play. All backgrounds should be kept flat, without projections of any kind to catch the strings of the marionettes as they pass. A caught string can be disastrous to temper and scene.

Imagine a dignified prince, about to kneel at the feet of the princess, and how disconcerting to everyone to have a string catch and land him sitting down—or pull him over backwards.

However, extra scenery can be added in a safe fashion. A stock outdoor scene can be changed greatly by a house, a golden castle, a huge tree, or a mountain. A golden castle in Fairyland is a lovely thing shining in the sunlight or moonlight.

Cut the castle out of cardboard. Make it high enough so that the tips of the towers reach nearly to the top of the screen. Glue the gold paper on it, painting the glue on the cardboard in crossbar pattern. On the gold outline the doors, windows, etc., using black paint or ink. Glue a piece of cloth (of inconspicuous color) back of the tower points. Have it long enough so that when you use the castle the cloth can be folded over the top of the screen and held by thumbtacks on the back. This method will hold your castle secure and flat against the background. It cannot pull forward during the performance and it is easy to shift quickly between acts. Trees and other additions to the scene may be added in similar fashion.

Designing a background for dancers gives you an opportunity to exercise all your ingenuity and artistic talent. Decide on the effect you wish to produce. If you wish the interest of your audience to be focused on a marionette with nothing whatever to distract the attention from the movement and color of the dancer, use velvet curtains of black or some neutral color for the background.

"The Flame" is very striking against black velvet draperies. She is dressed entirely in scarlet silk, and shoes and

"THE FLAME"

cape are of scarlet silk. Her hair is of scarlet. Earrings and shoe buckles flash scarlet fire as she wheels and leaps to music from Tschaikowsky's "Nutcracker Suite."

The black velvet curtains also serve as a background for a pantomime given by the Snow Flake Queen, nimble Jack Frost and his little icicle fairies. A pale blue screen casts a cold wintry light on the figures dancing and twirling to lovely music. Their costumes, all of white and sparkling silver, glisten through the softly descending snow.

For dancers who have filmy exquisite costumes and need a delicate background to carry out the tone of the dance,

NET BACKGROUND

illusive backgrounds can be made of white mosquito netting, embroidered with colored wool or silk. The gold screen shows through the net in a mysterious, alluring way.

Simple bold designs of trees or flowers cut out of colored materials and applied with short basting stitches to pieces of plain cloth make interesting backgrounds that are easy for anyone to make and a joy to handle.

Crêpe paper is one of the most satisfactory materials to

use for backgrounds; it wears well, (one of mine has been used at least a hundred times), it is inexpensive and comes in a wide range of colors. Dennison's fine grained crêpe paper in the flat package is the kind to use.

On the top edge of the foundation piece sew a strip of cloth a few inches wide to put your thumb-tacks through. Then appliqué the designs, using thread and needle instead of paste.

Vivid colors sewed on in large triangular folds made a smashing background for some stamping Russians.

APPLIQUED DESIGN OF CREPE PAPER

These appliquéd designs made of either cloth or crêpe paper are easier for the beginner than painted backgrounds. The appliqués can be cut out, basted on the foundation material, then tried out with the marionettes who are to use it.

If the impression is not right, in composition or color, the appliqués can be easily changed. It is good sport to work this way, discovering new effects in perspective and color.

Clowns can play against strong colors and design. A background suggestive of the circus is appropriate. Bright red elephants painted on a cream ground is attractive and funny.

For a pair of colorful gypsies, make a window-shade background with hills and flowers painted in bright colors. It is gay and lively.

PAINTED WINDOW-SHADE

When you wish to paint a background, you will find a window shade on a roller a satisfactory canvas. If you use coach paint, ground in Japan, it will go on without trouble.

The rolled-up scene packs well but is a little harder to handle on the stage. It is stiff and can not be tossed over your shoulder when you change scenes. It also requires careful thumb-tacking at the top.

Different mediums used for backgrounds give life, variety and freshness to each scene, that piques the interest of the audience.

Lighting.—After you have become expert and have

acquired a large stage you will probably not be able to resist buying a floodlight with color screens.

A colored light above, at the right, and white foot lights, make fascinating shadows in the folds of the costumes.

A red screen intensifies the warm colors in the scenes. Green or blue intensifies all cool colors.

Use orange for sunlight—pale blue for moonlight.

Rose can often give the finishing touch of mystery to a scene.

By using red footlights and white floodlight you produce a firelight glow.

Experiment with your lights to get the most interesting effect, then write it down so you will not forget.

For the small portable stage you can use a floor lamp for a flood or spotlight. Colored silks can be used in place of screens.

Music.—A music box is charming for marionettes and a small toy one is ideal for fairy music, but for general purposes phonograph music is the best.

The orthophonic recording is very beautiful. Use music such as Tschaikowsky's "Nutcracker Suite" played by the Philadelphia Symphony under the direction of Leopold Stokowski and recorded by the Victor Talking Machine Company. "Toy Symphony" by Joseph Hayden played by the Victor Concert Orchestra is splendid. The "Folk-Dance Music" (Burchenal-Crampton) such as the Russian "Kamarinskaia" by the Victor Military Band is invaluable. Music should be carefully selected. Keep trying different records until you find one that brings out the very best action of the marionettes.

When you have found the right music you will know it instantly, for the marionette will dance itself with very little thought on your part.

Stage Furniture.—Too much furniture clutters up the stage. A single chair and table can furnish a marionette room admirably. It must be made carefully to scale to look as though it really belonged.

You can find toy furniture in the shops but it is more fun to make it yourself and it will really be better on the stage than store things. If you are good at carpentering you will be able to turn out wonderful furniture of wood with very little trouble.

It is possible to make practical furniture out of pasteboard boxes. A square box with a piece of cardboard glued on to form a back makes an excellent chair. It is not hard to cut side pieces to make a wing chair out of a plain chair. Glue the side pieces to the box and overcast the back edges together. Make a turkey red cushion for the seat or a slip cover of some gay small-figured stuff.

The ordinary chair can be used for a throne by tying a decorative high back onto the ordinary back. The whole can be set on a low box.

A high oblong box can easily be cut to make a table—the drawing shows the way to cut the box. Put a piece of velvet over an oblong box, add a few pillows and you have a couch.

With colored crayons you can draw beautiful decorations on your tables and chairs. I use the crayons on wood as well as cardboard.

A very neat white picket fence was made with cardboard, scissors and crayon. If you wish to bend a cardboard fence, paste a piece of cloth about one and a half inches wide at the back of the corner to keep it from breaking.

The neat white board fence in the "Wishing Fairy" play is made of white cardboard—the top of the strip was cut in points and a dark blue crayon drew the openings. We made a gate and re-enforced it with strips of wood to hold the hinges.

An old stone well that joined part of the fence was crayoned on a paper box—flowers from the ten-cent store climb up the stone work. Jimmy and Susie climb up, too, and in one play fall into the well, through a trap door in the stage and into China!

Simple furniture and well-planned stage properties help a setting. By giving careful thought to each detail of a presentation, the whole impression cannot help but be one of completeness and perfection.

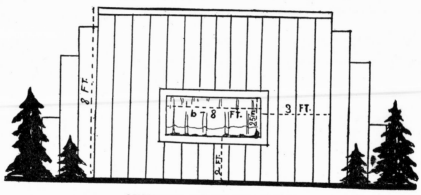

OUTDOOR STAGE FOR CAMP

Chapter VII

MARIONETTES IN CAMPS AND SCHOOLS

MARIONETTES are especially fascinating and worthwhile for children in camps or schools. Outdoor work in summer camps is particularly delightful.

Each child in camp can select something to do in connection with marionettes that will be particularly attractive to her. They involve such a variety of crafts that if a child has a special talent or liking for carpentry, sewing, painting, play-writing, or management, she can select the thing that suits her best or has the most lure for her.

Plans should be discussed before the work is started and the children should decide on two stage managers who will tend curtain, run the phonograph, change scenes, and see that the properties are in place on the stage for each act. If they like they can help make furniture and scenery and if the stage has not been built, help with its construction.

A permanent outdoor stage that is a great success is a wooden structure of simple design stained an inconspicuous greyish brown, the color of tree trunks. It stands outdoors through all weather without being harmed and is always ready for rehearsals and impromptu entertainments.

The stage is large enough so that five children can stand in a row to manipulate at once. The platform in back of the solid board background is wide enough for one child to pass another, and there are steps to the ground at each end. A rail running the full length of the platform keeps the children from falling off and is an ideal rack for the marionettes, the controls resting on long nails driven in the outside of the rail so that the marionettes hang out of the way.

Your stage floor can be two feet from the ground or higher and the back platform for the children to stand on must be the same level. The wooden background should be thirty inches high and three feet longer than your stage opening.

The stage opening or proscenium arch can be six or eight feet long but not higher than twenty-five inches. The front board protection should measure six feet high from the stage floor to the top and extend at least three feet each side of the stage opening.

The drop curtain can be tacked in folds to a flat wooden rod which is raised and lowered by ropes and an iron rod or pipe run through the bottom hem prevents the curtain from blowing when it is down.

As the floor of the stage is of wood little children can be used upon it with the marionettes. A real child going to sleep on the stage and having her toys (marionettes) come to life always delights the audience.

Younger children should be encouraged to make clowns because they are easiest to control and are not at all complicated to dress. Any number of clowns can be used in a regular entertainment and visitors are always fascinated by impromptu performances. Let the older ones decide on a play and if the play does not require many marionettes, so that there are some children left without characters to

"DUTCH"

make, have them make dancers—a Dutch couple, Spanish dancers, sailors, Indians—there are endless possibilities.

Keep an eye on the planning of the play. Too many children should not be back stage at once and the marionettes should pass each other as little as possible on the stage. If a character turns out particularly well you can give it more to do than you had planned at first. Sometimes one will walk unusually well, so keep him walking a great deal. It is hard sometimes for beginners to remember that the marionette's feet should be on the floor. They get so interested in what they are saying and in watching the other children who are working with them that up in the air flies the poor marionette. A pretty sure cure is to have the child who does it the most sit out front and help criticise the performance.

Some beautiful outdoor settings can be arranged on a camp stage, with rocks and moss, flowers and mushrooms. The background can have real-looking trees if you are where you can use flat hemlock branches. Black thread crisscrossed over it will hold it against the background so the strings of the marionettes will not catch. Groups of tiny ferns arranged at the front edge of the stage give a lovely effect.

One little play evolved in camp is a simple framework for numerous plays. The first scene was in one of the cabins and showed five little girls in their beds.

I hate to disillusion you but to help you I will confess that four of the little girls were nothing but heads fastened to pillows and the cots were cardboard boxes under covers.

Four little girls were good and one little girl was bad, they all chatted and giggled until taps was blown, then when all was quiet the bad little girl sat up, looked all about, then pulled out from under the covers a whacking big piece of blueberry pie! Presumably she ate every crumb, though the curtain fell too soon for us to see.

The second scene was in a magic street in wonderland. The little girl walking about in her pink pajamas and bedroom slippers met many strange people, weird animals and birds (this scene gave an opportunity to use a variety of characters), gypsies who passed through singing and dancing, a terrifying pirate with a wooden leg and his pet parrot that talked and squawked, and a magnificent magician who chanted in an outlandish language. The magician blew a tree flat on the ground with one breath, and as he waved it up again, the little girl jumped into the top of the tree which fell with a crash. CURTAIN!

The third scene was the same as the first—but the little girl was on the floor beside her bed, vowing never again to steal blueberry pie to eat after taps.

"The Pied Piper of Hamelin" is entrancing when given by marionettes.

Children in school, both boys and girls, enjoy making marionette children, and this play uses as many as you like. The poem should be read aloud to the audience as the play goes on. You will need to give the impression of great numbers of rats and children. It can be done by handling the marionettes in groups. For example, about five in one group, two in the next and three in the last—each group tied to a control that is simply one long stick. By prancing the rats across the stage and off—then entering as before and crossing again and again and again (varying the distance between the groups), the audience imagines *hundreds* of rats.

In schools the marionettes are an exhilarating help in many departments. They stimulate interest in art, crafts, history and language. Teachers and pupils love the genial marionettes.

Familiar fairy tales or legends when given in French take on an added fascination.

"Snow-White" is not at all difficult to adapt to marionettes. The little dwarfs especially are fun to make. Their rustic furniture, table and stools, were made of blocks of wood from the wood pile—the bark left on them.

"Red Riding Hood" also is easy to give and makes an interesting play, and many other familiar fairy tales and legends are easily adapted to marionettes.

To seek out interesting bits of history suitable for marionette plays or pageants to be given on special holidays is an alluring game.

Lessons in nutrition and hygiene can be given by rollicking clowns in such a blithe, bewitching way that they will never be forgotten.

Wherever there are children, in camp or school, marionettes furnish "something to do" that is full of joy and inspiration.

Two girls near Providence, Rhode Island have had a great deal of fun making marionettes and giving plays.

They saw one of my entertainments and asked very intelligent questions, then went enthusiastically to work and in less than twenty-four hours each had a good workable marionette; one had made the whole thing and the other had strung up a very limber cloth doll. The next I heard of them they were giving regular shows in a barn and in the school and town hall.

A group of business women in Portland, Maine wished to put on a novel sketch for the entertainment of visiting women in town for the Business Women's Convention. They had their idea and sent one woman to me for a lesson— I'm sure the entertainment was "novel" and amusing, for their idea was full of humor.

Girl Scout troops and Y. W. C. A. girls have found that the marionettes are great sport and the entertainments are money raisers—they always draw a large crowd.

Little groups of children from ten to fourteen years old in several villages and cities have formed clubs to make marionettes. They meet at each other's houses to plan and sew and often the resultant entertainments are so interesting that they are invited to give them at school.

Women's Clubs, too, are becoming interested; some have sent groups or a clever member for instruction. They attempt more dramatic serious plays usually.

But it doesn't much matter *why* or where you undertake marionette-making—you will find the work fascinating.

Chapter VIII

PRESENTING THE PROGRAM

WHEN giving a program professionally I have found
that the fewer people behind the scenes, the less con-
fusion. Unless it is a stupendous production with a great
many characters to be kept moving on the stage at once, two
operators can successfully put on a complete show.

I find that speaking all the lines myself (changing my
voice for the different characters) gives a smoothness to
the presentation that is impossible to obtain in any other
way. Voices of marionettes should never be "top heavy,"
so to speak. A six-foot male voice used for a two-foot puppet unless carefully done is apt to make the audience more
conscious of the six-foot male than the character on the
stage.

If one person speaks the lines, cues are not missed, no
matter what the accidents. My assistant is my extra brain
and extra hands; together we are able to do everything
needful. I carry on the voice while she hops up and down,
running the music, bringing in new characters and manipulating when several are on the stage at once. She snores
sonorously for the giant and sings for Jimmy but otherwise
her voice runs along something like this, "Keep talking a
little longer, I can't start this phonograph." "You haven't

59

mentioned the fairy—don't forget," and "Don't step back on the dog!"

It is possible when you have absolute control of a play to give it for children two years old, using simple words, repeating important lines in more than one way, and depending as far as possible on the action to tell the story. For older children you can use restraint or quicken the whole feeling of the play.

As you sit ready behind the curtains you have an opportunity to gauge your audience. By listening carefully you will be able to judge their tempo and you will know whether they will appreciate a subtle quiet performance or a quick, smart presentation of the play.

Little children adore having their names mentioned by the clown. A list of their names can be made beforehand. You can pick up other information about new clothes, haircuts, etc., by listening to their chatter. The fact that the clown has known a child's name has often, in the child's mind, outlived the memory of the play.

We have had some interesting experiences. Once in giving a new play—and because it was new, being very intent on what we were doing—a little hand reached in and took hold of the little boy marionette! The audience roared and we had to stop short—feeling rather dazed. Finally we thought it time to go on with the play and as no one in the audience of several hundred had taken the child away we spoke gently—"You had better go back now." A little girl about four years old poked her head in on the stage and discovered us up above. She was as dazed as we were.

We spoke a little more decidedly but she still looked us all over. Finally someone took her away. She had been so engrossed with the play that she had forgotten the audience and walked up to see whether the little people were alive or not.

Another time I had been asked to explain how the marionettes worked, so after the play was over, although it is hard for me to talk when seen, I went out front with a clown and told all about it. When I was through a little boy piped up—"Yes—but how did he do it when he did it himself?" After another performance a child was heard telling her father, "It was a very *little* man but a real man."

Children often exclaim during the play—and sometimes cry. I had to change the ending of one play and have the dragon un-eat the children explaining that "it was just a joke and he hadn't any teeth anyhow."

To pack the marionettes so they will not tangle, lay one in the bottom of the suitcase (if you use a suitcase), put a piece of tissue paper over it, then fold the control and strings on top of this and cover with tissue. And so on, layer after layer. I always carry my most prized marionettes this way and they keep fresh and uncrushed.

I allow a full half-hour for setting up the small stage and arranging the marionettes and a full hour for the large stage. When you arrive at the place where you are to give the entertainment try out your electric connection as soon as possible. I carry a plug that screws into a light socket. Sometimes if the outlet is too far away, you can plug into a lamp. Try out the phonograph if you have not brought your own. Carry "extra loud" needles with you, the kind that does not need to be changed every time. Of course take your own records.

For a smoothly running performance you should allow plenty of time for so placing the marionettes that they can be grasped quickly by the control without tangling themselves or knocking another one down. If one does accidentally fall, and improvising talk and action on the stage will not cover the delay, you will have to drop the curtain. You can usually avoid accidents by ingenuity beforehand. One of my tricks is to carry with me a couple of yards of black paper muslin and a dozen brass curtain hooks that are made like large safety pins with a hook attached. Very often in private homes we are backed up against curtains and pressed for room but with push pins and these safety pins it is possible to make a splendid rack for the marionettes without injuring hangings. It can be put over the family portrait or hung from the moulding. It is a valuable help and takes up very little room when packed.

Backgrounds can often be thumbtacked in place on the stage, one over another. Write down the order of your program so that there will be no misunderstanding.

From experience I have found the following arrangement of a program the most satisfactory:

I open with one clown on the stage sitting perfectly still upon a small stool. The phonograph is playing some attractive popular music. The clown raises his head, then a hand, keeps time with his foot, rises, strikes attitudes, keeps time with both hands, breaks into a dance and finishes his

"SITTING PERFECTLY STILL"

act standing on his hands. He exits by a wild scramble up and over the background screen. The audience is delighted at the simplest movement of the head or hand—they even like him motionless—so build up his little act gradually and it is more effective than starting in at full speed.

Beginning with a clown gives late comers a chance to rustle in and settle themselves without interrupting too much and also gives the children a chance to ask their parents all the questions they can think up.

Following the dance, the clown announces the next number on the program and then shouts for the curtain to come down—"Easy there, boys—easy—easy does it!" Sometimes he gets caught by the curtain as he tries to ease it down and the children go into gales of laughter.

"The next number on the program, ladies and gentlemen," is usually a dancer. If a long program is desired I give several different dancers with a different background for each. Quaint dancers are always well applauded and tempestuous Russians are very popular.

The clown next announces a short intermission (usually five or six minutes) "before the play, ladies and gentlemen, in three scenes—*three* scenes, ladies and gentlemen!"

Then with the dancers out of our way—laid in the suitcase if possible as they come off the stage—we give a final look about to see that all is shipshape—take a long breath and raise the curtain for the play.

Very often an audience is so stimulating that you think up new lines, and every time you do and the audience *laughs,* store that bit away and use it the next time.

After the curtain goes down on the last act, raise it again as quickly as possible and reach out and take hold of the hand of the marionette on the stage.

The audience will gasp because your hand will look like a giant hand.

When watching the small performers, people lose their sense of proportion and a human hand appearing so huge is a terrific jolt.

At the end of the play the children usually are eager to see how the manipulating is done and they get a great thrill out of peeping behind the scenes, so let them come back whenever it is possible—their comments are priceless. You will feel well paid for having done your best.

Chapter IX

MAKING YOUR OWN PLAYS

MAKING up plays yourself even though they are not dramatically perfect, gives you a thrilling sense of closeness to the marionettes that cannot possibly be felt when an effort is being made to interpret the ideas of another.

If you cannot think clearly at first, when you attempt to make a play, remember that there is nothing new under the sun—magic and dreams have always cast their spell.

Animals, little wild creatures and insects of the woods or fields, furnish abundant ideas for imaginative plays. Rabbits are particularly appealing, their long ears are so expressive. Frogs, mosquitoes, spiders and bumble bees are good comedians.

Little woods-people, dryads and elves have that whimsical quality so characteristic of a marionette and so difficult for a human actor to portray.

The same characters can be used over and over in an endless number of beautiful adventures—a fairy riding a dragon-fly steed; a dryad appearing from its tree; a frog croaking in a swamp. The woods are full of marvelous play material.

At Christmas time, the real Christmas story can be

simply and reverently presented with marionettes. If carefully planned and the restrained motion necessary in such a scene thoroughly rehearsed, then with subdued lighting the production should be full of a rare spiritual beauty.

If you wish to give a Christmas entertainment and have not time to make an appropriate play, you can get your Christmas spirit with the aid of a jolly Santa Claus. He can give a prologue explaining that the play you are about to give is one of his Christmas books come to life, for the children.

A tiny little clown or a live doll jumping down from a pack on his back, to dance and sing for Santa Claus, is surprising.

The audience feels an instant familiar friendliness for a marionette Santa Claus. He is another character of fancy more easily portrayed by marionette than man.

A wintry pantomime with a snowman for a hero is amusing and easily arranged. Music and children, a gay dance before the snowman that they have just completed, the departure of the children and the melting of the snowman. He is made of turkish toweling; bits of odd-shaped black velvet make the coal-like eyes, nose, mouth and buttons, and a black satin hat and a stick in his hand give the final touch. As the body is hollow and held in shape by two wire hoops, he melts convincingly.

A small trap door in the stage is a great asset. Genii rise up out of the floor upsetting furniture; little boys can catch quantities of fish, each larger than the last and sometimes catch other things besides, frogs or mermaids. A magic jewel tree showing first a tiny tip, grows under the charm of a magician's fan until the gorgeous sparkling branches reach the sky—and if you wish, the earth can slowly swallow it up once more.

A magic carpet is simply a square piece of cardboard under a larger square of rug-like material. Strings going through the carpet to fasten in the corners of the cardboard carry the magic carpet. Fasten all four strings to one stick the same length as your square of cardboard.

If you wish a marionette to walk a tight-rope, place two black pins in each foot to keep him from slipping off the rope. The audience will gasp most satisfactorily when he teeters and cheer enthusiastically when he reaches his goal.

Just one clown, a beginner's clown, can furnish a whole evening of entertainment if you do not wish to start with a play.

Walk him across the room or stage if you have one— whistle a tune for him. If you have trouble with your whistling so much the better. He may be shy, he may be nonchalant but he will surely be captivating.

Find something with which he can play. A board with one end resting on a block provides material for good clowning.

The clown walks around the board—looking it over. His attempts to walk up it are not very successful at first but he finally succeeds in reaching the end—he makes preparations for a great leap but changes his mind and walks back, but sits on the end swinging his feet—gazes at the ground, then at the audience. At last he stands erect and makes a quick leap—thump! He lands sitting down! He staggers around examining the board from all angles, then runs away as hard as he can go.

This is just a suggestion. When you have once put him through a few tricks ideas will come as fast as you can work.

Little children are delighted with a scene between a clown and a Jack-in-the-Box. Prepare the Jack-in-the-Box by breaking Jack loose from the box. Remove the spring and fasten a weight to the bottom of Jack to keep him from coming entirely out of the box. Attach a string to the lid of the box and two strings to Jack's head.

The play can go something like this:

The curtain rises on Clown seated on the floor, leaning in a relaxed position against the box. He snores at intervals. The Lid of the box lifts a little—then closes—Clown snores.

Lid of the box opens wider—Jack's head appears—he gazes about.

Clown snores.

Lid closes.

Lid of box opens wide as Jack pops up and says—BOO!

Clown is disturbed but snores again.

Jack pops up and says—BOO!!

Clown jumps in his sleep—moves an arm or leg.

Jack pops up and says—BOO!!!

Clown jumps to his feet and looks all around—everywhere but at the box. While he is furthest away and back to the box Jack pops up again and says—BOO! BOO!! BOO!!!

Clown spies him—makes a dash for him but the lid closes.

Clown walks all around the box, examining it closely.

Lid starts to open and Clown jumps as though to grab Jack.

Lid closes.

Clown has a happy thought—he will hold Jack a prisoner. He sits on the box with his face away from the audience, then rises and sits face to the audience—kicking feet happily.

Gay music starts off stage.

Clown listens a few moments—keeps time with his hands then with his feet. Finally he can resist music no longer—he rises and dances ecstatically.

Jack slowly opens the box and happily keeps time to the music with his head.

Clown dances over to him and sits on the floor beside him.

Jack leans toward him. They are friends!

CURTAIN

Incidents from Chinese myths woven together form an attractive, colorful play. Records of Chinese music can be bought for it.

Here is a suggestion for a play of this type:

Cast.—The Emperor, his daughter, his servant, a traveling wizard and a monkey.

The Emperor seated on his throne, mourns the loss of

his beloved daughter. The servant tells him of a Wizard outside the gate. The people tell wonderful tales of him—if he strikes a stone with his staff the stone comes to life! If he strikes a cow with his staff the cow falls dead! If he washes his red shirt in the river the water boils!

Perhaps he can help cheer the Emperor!

The Wizard is admitted—music sounds at a wave of his staff! The Wizard dances for the Emperor—the Emperor has seen better dancers. The Wizard raises a jewel tree from the earth—the Emperor is not astonished. The Wizard calls down snow from heaven—the Emperor has seen snow. The Wizard brings red snow—the Emperor is not impressed. (The snow is tissue paper cut in fine pieces.) The Wizard calls down the monkey-god Sum, who capers about in glee and climbs a rope raised stiff in the air by the Wizard's magic—and the help of a black thread!

Still the Emperor is disconsolate—he berates the Wizard.

"One does no more than one must to be amusing!" says the Wizard.

Finally he tells the Emperor that he knows where his daughter is hidden—in the Palace of the Sun God. He consents to bring her to earth on a ray of light, but the Emperor must promise not to touch her or speak to her.

Music is heard.

The little Chinese princess comes slowly dancing down on a diagonal ray of light—dances a few moments and then trips back to heaven—to the despair of her father! (The ray of light is a silver ribbon about an eighth of an inch wide. It lies flat on the floor of the stage, one end is fast-

ened to the floor at the extreme right, the other end, when
needed, is raised by a black thread.)

The Emperor promises the Wizard fields, money, jewels
if he will bring his daughter back to stay—but the Wizard
can get these things for himself with his magic.

At last he bargains with the Emperor—if he will have
him for a son-in-law, then indeed he will bring the Princess
back once more. The Emperor grants his wish.

The music is heard once more.

The ray of light quivers—the Princess trips slowly down
to earth and dances with the Wizard. At the conclusion
of the dance they kneel at the feet of the Emperor for his
blessing. And then the curtain falls.

This can be a lavish scene resplendent with radiant
color and full of dramatic action.

An appropriate background would be a huge green
dragon against dull gold.

The costumes should be of the most gorgeous silks and
embroideries, the colors intense jade green, yellow, purple,
scarlet and gold.

The jewel tree sparkles and flashes with brilliant fire as
the light strikes the hundreds of emeralds and diamonds.

Fantastic Chinese music completes the bizarre con-
coction.

Try doing a play before you try writing one—none of
mine were written down until they were two years old. I
changed them nearly every time I gave them. I was so
tickled when I thought of a see-saw for Jimmy and Susie
in "The Wishing Fairy."

Different plays can be written for Jimmy and Susie—
I have taken them to China and I expect to take them to
visit Eskimos. Why don't you take them traveling through
the sky to call on the man in the moon?

FIVE PLAYS FOR MARIONETTES

THE ADVENTURES OF BETTY

By Edith Flack Ackley

A one-act play for marionettes that can be given by one person.

Characters: Betty, her mother, Bill Sure-Enough, the Lion, the Gypsy, the Goose, the Little Live Doll and two fairies.

A hook of double wire is fastened to the left upright to hold the control of Betty until almost the end of the act. Her hands can be raised and her head turned whenever you have one hand free to lift the strings.

The scene is laid in the woods. Betty is seated on a log at the right, her mother with a basket on her arm stands facing her.

Betty: Mother, I cannot go another step! My feet are so tired they just won't go on walking! What shall I do?

Mother: Dear! Dear! Won't you try again, Betty! We have only half a mile further to go! I want Jane to have these nice little cakes I have baked, and as she has been ill I think a surprise would please her. Please try again, Betty.

Betty: Mother, I cannot climb over one more stick or stone! Let me stay here to rest and you go on to Jane's house.

Mother: Oh, Betty, I don't like to leave you here alone—you might wander off and get lost.

Betty: No, Mother, I'll not wander away. I promise to stay right in this very place until you come back and I'm not the least bit afraid of being alone in the woods. You go along and take the cakes to Jane and don't worry about me.

Mother: All right, dear—I'll hurry as fast as I can and before the sun sets I'll be back with you.

Betty: (as mother exits left) Give Janie my love, Mother. Tell her to get well soon!

Mother: (off stage) Goodbye, Betty dear—Goodbye.

Betty: Goodbye—goodbye, Mother! (a pause) How still it is here in the woods now Mother has gone. It is rather lonely with no one to talk to. I wonder how far she has gone by this time—maybe she can walk faster without me.

Voice: Hello—Hello! What do I see! It looks like an honest-to-goodness child!

Betty: Who is it? Where are you—why don't you come where I can see you?

Voice: Not so many questions at once, my child. It sounds very rude!

Bill Sure-Enough, an orange-haired, bewhiskered little dwarf, bounces to the ground.

Bill Sure-Enough: What do you think you are doing here, little girl?

Betty: I don't just *think* I'm doing something here. I *know* what I'm doing here.

Bill Sure-Enough: I don't see the difference but you didn't answer my question—girls always argue instead of answering a question!

Betty: No, we don't, either—but I've forgotten what it was you asked.

Bill Sure-Enough: (*patiently and slowly*) What do you think you are doing out here in my woods?

Betty: Oh! Are these your woods? I thought they belonged to——

Bill Sure-Enough: Answer my question—answer my question!

Betty: Well, it was a *stupid* question! I should think you could see for yourself that I am sitting on a log resting. My mother will come for me soon, but—do tell me your name!

Bill: Bill Sure-Enough!

Betty: (*laughing heartily*) Bill Sure-Enough! That's a funny name.

Bill: Nothing funny about that!

Betty: Of course there is—why are you called *Sure-Enough*? There's no sense to that.

Bill: Of course there is sense to that—Sure-Enough I'm here and Sure-Enough I'm gone!

(*Saying which he jumps up out of sight.*)

Betty: Oh, come back! Come back!

Bill's voice: I like it better here in the tree.

Betty: Oh, come back, please do! I am so lonesome here
waiting for my mother.

Bill: (jumping down) Well, if you are so lonesome, why
don't you do something about it?

Betty: What can I do?

Bill: Wish for something to amuse you! I'll make a wish
for you if you like—I'll wish for a lion! I like lions.

(Bill springs up out of sight.)

Betty: Oh, Bill! Bill! I am afraid of lions! Don't wish
for a lion!

*(Roars are heard and Lion enters, galloping and waving
tail. Betty raises her hands in fright as he comes toward
her, but the Lion bounds away again and prances about
the stage roaring.)*

Betty: Bill, Bill, send him away!

(The Lion departs instantly.)

Bill: (jumping down) How did you like that?

Betty: Well, he didn't eat me, but I'm glad you wished him
away.

Bill: You think of something to wish for now.

Betty: Oh *I* know—I'd like a gypsy to dance for me!

Bill: All right! Watch for a gypsy.

Bill: (jumping up and down)

> One for a penny
> Two for a show
> Three to make ready
> And four to go!

(Bill disappears above.)

Music (*such as "Toy Symphony"*).   Gypsy enters and dances engagingly for Betty, she dancing off before the music stops.

Betty: Oh, Bill, Bill!   That was lovely.   I have another thought, too, Bill!

Bill: (*jumping down*)   Let's hear it, Betty.

Betty: Do you know what I'd like best of all?   To see a little live doll—one from a store that talks and dances!

Bill: That is too hard for me, Betty.   I couldn't wish hard enough, but I'll tell you what I'll do—I'll wish for a great white goose; she will bring you a doll from the store.

Betty: Bill, you are marvelous!   Hurry up and wish!

Bill: All right.   Sure enough I will.   Off I go to my tree!

(*Bill jumps up out of sight once more as Goose appears with the live doll.*)

Goose: Here she is—it was a very long trip.

Live Doll: Let me off!   Oh, let me off!   Oh, my poor dress! and my bonnet is all askew!

(*She hops off and the Goose flies away.*)

Live Doll: (*going over to Betty and bowing to her*)   Are you the little girl who wished to see a beautiful doll? Well, here I am.   Now what can I do for you?

Betty: Sing for me, won't you please?   Do you know any songs?

Live Doll: Certainly I know some songs.   I know "Bobby Shafto's gone to sea."   Shall I sing it for you?

Betty: Please do.   I've never heard it.

(*Live Doll sings in a tiny voice the song "Bobby Shafto."*)

Live Doll: Shall I sing you another?

Betty: Oh, yes, I'd love to hear another.

Live Doll: "Cock-a-doodle-doo my dame has lost her shoe," etc.

(*She dances as she sings.*)

Betty: Oh, little live doll, won't you stay and go home to live with me? I love you so dearly.

Live Doll: Where do you live?

Betty: You can just see the top of the roof of our red barn if you will stand over here by me. We have a lovely home, and we have chickens and kittens and dogs—oh, *do* come home with me!

Live Doll: Great live chickens and kittens and dogs! Oh, mercy me, how terrible! I couldn't think of such a thing! I am sure I'd be homesick. I'd miss my beautiful box trimmed with paper lace, and my covers of tissue! I think I'd better be leaving AT ONCE!

(*The Goose flies down.*)

Goose: Hop on, my dear, hop on; you'll be back in your store in a jiffy.

Betty: Goodbye, little doll—goodbye!

Live Doll: Goodbye, little girl. (*Exit on Goose.*)

(*A pause. Then Goose returns.*)

Betty: (*rising*) Oh, thank you so much! What a wonderful way to travel! You couldn't possibly take *me* home, could you?

Goose: But Bill says that you are waiting for your mother. Won't she worry to find you gone?

Betty: I'm afraid she would. What shall we do about it?

Goose: Don't worry, I'll take you home and Bill can watch for your mother to come. He will explain to her. You can surprise her by having the supper ready on the table. Jump on—jump on!

Betty: (Seating herself on the back of the Goose) Oh! Oh! Oh!
(They fly off.)

Scene II.

Music is Playing.
Betty is asleep on the ground—her head resting against the log of wood on which she had been sitting.
Two fairies fly through the air dipping and twirling until the music ceases.

First Fairy: We have given her a wonderful dream! Don't you think she will be pleased, sister?

Second Fairy: Let's wake her now!
(They dart about her.)

First Fairy: Come! hurry away—I hear her mother coming.

Mother's Voice: Betty—Betty, I am coming.
(Mother enters.)

Mother: Betty—Betty—Why, the child is sound asleep! Wake up! wake up! The sun is setting! We must hurry home!

Betty: (in a sleepy voice) Oh, Mother, did you see the lion?

Mother: Lion! Mercy, Betty, of course I didn't! There are no lions in these woods.

Betty: That is strange. I was sure I saw a lion. Did you meet the gypsy, Mother, or the goose?

Mother: You most certainly have been dreaming—come, child, it is time to go.

(She starts off.)

Betty: (lingering behind) It didn't seem like a dream—I did like Bill Sure-Enough so much! I think I'll call and see if he hears me.

Mother: (off stage) Come, Betty, come!

Betty: (walking after Mother, turns and calls up to Bill) Bill! Oh, Bill Sure-Enough! Goodbye!

Bill's Voice: (very faint) Goodbye, Betty.

Betty: Oh, I was right. There *is* a Bill!

(Betty exits.)

CURTAIN

(THE WISHING FAIRY) ACT I

THE WISHING FAIRY

A play for marionettes, in three scenes.

Characters: Jimmy, Susie, their mother, their dog, the Wishing Fairy, the Giant, his daughter, his pet elephant, a snake and a witch.

Scene I. Jimmy's and Susie's back yard, with an outdoor back-drop; white fence across back stage. Yellow floodlight.

When curtain rises Jimmy and Susie are on see-saw, center back, singing:

> See-saw, Marjorie Daw,
> Jennie shall have a new master;
> She shall have but a penny a day
> Because she can't work any faster.

Jimmy: Can't you sing any better than that, Susie? That's terrible singing!

Susie: Nothing the matter with that singing, Jimmy Whitmarsh!

Jimmy: Aw, you sing just like a girl!

Susie: Well, I *am* a girl! Anyway, you have a smudge on your nose!

Jimmy: I have not, but you have egg on your apron!

Susie: You are horrid, Jimmy.

Susie: (*as Jimmy thumps see-saw*) Don't thump so, Jimmy; it hurts!

Jimmy: (*holding her up in the air*) Well, how do you like that?

Susie: (*kicking*) You let me down, Jimmy Whitmarsh! Let me down! Let me down! I'll tell Mother on you, I'll tell her how mean you are to me.

Jimmy: All right, go ahead tell her, Tattle Tale Susie! Tattle Tale Susie! Tattle Tale Susie!

Susie: Mother! Mother!

Mother: (*entering from right*) What's all this? What's the trouble, children?

Children: (*rapidly*)

It's Jimmy, Mother.

Susie's cross.

No; it's Jimmy, he's mean, Mother.

Susie's an old cross patch.

Mother: Children, children, be quiet a minute! Something must be the matter. Dear, dear, bless my soul! Susie, look at me! (*She examines Susie's face carefully.*) Let me see the back of your neck. (*Susie drops head forward so her mother can see.*) Everything seems all right. (*She goes to Jimmy, examining him in same way.*) No, I don't see any spots or speckles; it can't be chicken pox or measles. *(Facing audience)* I wonder if it can't be mumps or whooping cough. Oh, I hope not! Maybe they are just hungry. Are you hungry, children?

Jimmy: What are we going to have for supper, Mother? Something good?

Mother: Of course it's good, Jimmy? *(slowly and distinctly)* You are going to have cereal, and baked apple.

Jimmy: Oh, Mother, we are so tired of cereal and apples.

Susie: And do we have to have milk again tonight? We are so tired of milk!

Mother: Why yes, nice, fresh milk, Susie. It's so good.

Susie: Oh, Mother, all our suppers have milk!

Mother: Well, bless my soul, you don't sound like my children at all. I am going in the house. I can't imagine what the trouble is. *(goes off right, talking)* I do hope they aren't going to be sick!

Susie: You were horrid to Mother, Jimmy.

Jimmy: So were you, Susie.

Susie: Not as horrid as you, Jimmy. I should think she'd get tired of having you for a son!

Jimmy: If you would just keep still a minute, Susie, I could say something.

Susie: Well, you are doing as much talking as I am. What is it?

Jimmy: You don't know how to keep still! I just wanted to ask you if you had seen Mabel's new book with the giants in it. Wouldn't you like to see a real giant, Susie?

Susie: No, I don't think so.

Jimmy: Oh, I would. I get sick and tired of going to school every day, and Sunday School on Sundays and everything. I wish we could have a change.

Dog: (*entering right*) Woof, Woof, Woof.

Jimmy: Well, you poor old thing, what's the matter with you?

Susie: Get away from me, you are all wet! You have been in the brook again!

Dog: (*goes on barking, then howls.*)

Susie: What's the matter with him, Jimmy?

Jimmy: Just old, I guess. Susie, maybe he'll have to be shot.

Susie: He acts as though he heard something or saw something strange.

Dog: (*exits, howling, right.*)

Flute or bird is heard.

Susie: There, I heard something!

Jimmy: I did too!

Fairy flies down.

Jimmy: Oh, Susie, look, look, there is a fairy!
How do you do, Miss Fairy?

Fairy: How do you do, children. I am a Wishing Fairy. I heard you wish, Jimmy! You would like to see a giant?

Jimmy: Oh, yes, we would—can you take us, Miss Fairy?

Fairy: Yes, I can take you to see a huge giant. Can you be ready in about five minutes?

Jimmy: Oh, yes, we will be ready!

Fairy flies away.

Jimmy: Hurry back, Miss Fairy. Oh, Susie, won't that be wonderful! Aren't you glad, Susie?

Susie: (sounding very much frightened) I don't know, Jimmy! Will he be very terrible?

Jimmy: (see-sawing as curtain comes down, in loud manly voice) I'll take care of you! Don't be a 'fraid cat, Susie.

CURTAIN

Scene II

The Giant's Home

*Paisley back-drop, table and chair at left of center,
candlestick on table.*
Giant seated, snoring, head forward, arm on table.
Snake flat on floor at right.

Jimmy: (*legs shaking*) My, he is big! (*turns and calls
in a shaking voice to Susie, off stage, right*) Come on,
Susie, it's all right, this is the place, don't be a 'fraid cat!
He stands center right, as Susie enters.
Jimmy: Don't let your knees shake, Susie. It's all right!
Susie: My knees aren't shaking. Your knees are shaking.
Jimmy: No, my feet are cold, that's all.
Susie: That is such a terrible noise, Jimmy!
Jimmy: Sure it is, but it's just snoring. He's a giant, re-
member.

Susie: (*walks over and looks at Giant*) What big boots he has Jimmy. I'm afraid of him.
(*Jimmy goes over to table and starts climbing up with grunts and groans.*)

Susie: Jimmy Whitmarsh, what are you doing? You get down, I tell you.

Jimmy: Don't nag, Susie. I'm all right. I can see better up here. (*sits on table, swinging leg*) Say Susie, this will be wonderful to tell the children. (*He moves and knocks candlestick off table, waking Giant.*)

Susie: Now see what you've done! Oh! Oh! Oh!
(*Children stand center back.*)
(*Giant rises, stretches, shakes himself awake, sees the children. Sits again.*)

Giant: (*in terrific voice*) What are you doing here, eh?

Jimmy: You talk to him, Susie.

Susie: I don't want to. You do it, Jimmy.

Jimmy: Oh, go on, you usually talk enough! Say something.

Giant: WELL?

Susie: (*hesitating*) Oh, we just thought we'd like to see a giant, so we came to call on you.

Giant: And now that you see me, what do you think of me? Eh?
(*They jump whenever the Giant says, "Eh."*)

Susie: Well, you have very large ears, Mr. Giant!

Giant: (*shaking his hand at Susie*) Large ears? And do you know why I have such large ears, young lady? Be-

cause, when I was a little boy—I—would not—WASH
—THEM!!

Susie: Oh, did you hear that, Jimmy? Maybe that is why
Mother is so fussy when we wash our ears.
(Giant begins to doze.)

Jimmy: Talk some more, Susie, he is going to sleep.

Susie: Please don't go to sleep, Mr. Giant!

Giant: Sleep? Don't you know that the nights aren't long
enough for giants? They were made for ordinary people. Let me sleep.

Susie: What shall I talk about, Jimmy?

Jimmy: Tell him about our dog. Maybe he has a pet. Ask
him.

Susie: We have an old black dog, Mr. Giant. Have you
any pets?

Giant: Pets! A dog! No, I wouldn't have a dog, but I
have a pet! He is a baby now, but when he grows up
he will be a beauty!

Susie: Oh, please call him. What is his name?

Giant: His name is Flaps. He can do his tricks for you.
Flaps, Flaps—*(still louder)* FLAPS.
(Music of a Highland Fling starts off stage.)

Giant: Flaps, come, do your tricks!

Susie: Oh! a baby, Jimmy! Won't that be cunning!
Maybe it is a kitten.

Jimmy: Oh, no, he wouldn't have a kitten. Maybe it is a
goat. Oh, Susie, look!
(The elephant comes in from the right, dances, flaps one

*ear and then the other, goes round and round, stands on head
and waves tail while the children squeal and try to get out of
his way.   The Giant calls out now and then—"Round and
round, Flaps—Earn your breakfast, Flaps!"   Elephant exits
right.)*

Jimmy: Well, I'm glad he has gone.   He will be quite a pet
when he grows up.   Say, Susie, I'm hungry.   I wonder
if he has anything to eat.   You ask him, Susie.

Susie: What do you feed your pet, Mr. Giant?

Giant: Peanuts—fresh ones, roasted ones, salted ones!   Peanuts, of course!

Susie: You don't happen to have anything for us to eat, do
you, Mr. Giant?

Giant: Let me think, let me think!   I'll ask my daughter.
Mehitable, Mehitable!

*Mehitable: (entering left if big stage is used, but calling
from off stage if space is limited)*   Yes, Father?

Giant: Have we a drumstick left from the roast ostrich we
had last night, Mehitable?

Mehitable: I'll see, Father.   *(Exits left.)*

Susie: Oh, Jimmy, wouldn't that be too tough?

Jimmy: Goodness yes, Susie.

Mehitable: (calling from off stage)   It's all gone, Father,
but you might send out that last cobra.

Giant: Yes, Mehitable, I'll send it. *(makes hissing noise at
snake and snake slithers across stage, up across table
and out left)*

Giant: (while snake is moving)   Here he comes!   Fry it
brown and save the head for me, Mehitable.

Mehitable: (*off stage*) Yes, Father.

(*Children exclaim and squeal as snake passes.*)

Susie: Oh, Jimmy, I don't think I want to eat a snake.

Jimmy: Neither do I, Susie.

Mehitable: (*entering left*) Father, oh, Father, I have an idea!

(*She whispers loudly to Father but no words are distinguishable.*)

Giant: (*slowly*) Fine, Mehitable, fine! We'll have the little boy *ROASTED* and the little girl *CREAMED ON TOAST!* Yum, yum, yum, yum! (*Mehitable exits left while Giant is talking. He rubs his stomach.*) Build up the fire, Mehitable! Yum, yum, yum, yum! That's something to dream about! Call me when you're ready, Mehitable!

(*Children shaking, Susie crying, Giant dozes.*)

Susie: Oh, Jimmy, I don't want to be eaten—let's go away.

Jimmy: All right, Susie, come this way. (*starts right*)

Susie: Oh, no, Jimmy!

Jimmy: Why not? Come on!

Susie: No, that elephant is there and he will step on us.

Jimmy: Then come this way. Hurry while he sleeps!

Susie: No, Jimmy, no! Mehitable is there—she would cook us. Oh, what can we do! I wish we were home!

Jimmy: Well, I wish I had you home, Susie!

(*Fairy bugle is heard.*)

Jimmy: There—it's all right, Susie. There is the Fairy. She will take us home again. Don't be scared, Susie— I said I'd take care of you!

(Fairy flies down, floats about and alights at right. Children rush up to her.)

Jimmy: Oh, we are glad to see you, Miss Fairy. Susie would like to go home. Will you please take us?

Susie: (falling on knees) Oh, *please* take us home!

Fairy: Well—do you know it's very hard to *undo* a thing. I don't believe I can take you home!

Jimmy: What! You can't take us home!

Susie: (weeping) Oh, please take us home!

Jimmy: Yes; Mother will worry terribly and Susie really wishes to go right now.

Fairy: Let me see, there is one thing I can do—I can ask a friend of mine if she will take you.

Jimmy: Oh, please do and won't you hurry?

Susie: Do tell her to come before he wakes up.

Fairy: Very well. I'll find her as fast as I can. *(flies off)*

Susie: Oh, Jimmy, I hope he sleeps! I hope she hurries!

(SWISH! Witch flies in on a broomstick—right center front.)

Susie: Oh, Jimmy, she is a witch! *(turning to witch)* Aren't you a witch?

Witch: Of course I'm a witch! Hurry up and climb on, if I'm to take you home.

Susie: Oh my—I never can climb on—I'm afraid!

Jimmy: (climbs on broomstick in back of witch) Climb on, Susie! Of course you can do it.

Susie: (climbs on in front of witch) We'll fall off!

Witch: No, you won't. I've been riding this broomstick 495 years and I haven't fallen off yet!

Susie: Oh, it's moving! I'm afraid!

Jimmy: Hold on tight, Susie!

Susie: Oh, we are going so high, Jimmy!

(Voices fade away. Giant snores.)

CURTAIN

SUSIE AND JIMMIE

Scene III

Scene same as I, with yellow floodlight.

Jimmy: It's good to be home again, Susie!

Susie: Goodness, yes! Do you know, Jimmy, I think it would be better not to tell Mother. She'd feel so dreadful to think of you being roasted.

Jimmy: And you creamed on toast, Susie—Oh I can never eat creamed chicken again, I know! And Susie, I don't believe we'd better tell the children at school either—they'd never believe it.

Susie: That's a good idea, Jimmy.

Jimmy: There is Mother coming, Susie. *(calls in pleasant voice)* Oh, Mother, Mother!

Mother: *(enters as before)* Well, children, do you feel happier?

94

Jimmy: Oh, we feel *hungrier,* Mother, that's what we feel. Did you say baked apples, Mother?

Susie: And milk, Mother? I could just drink quarts.

Mother: I'm so glad! Yes—plenty of milk and muffins too, with honey!

Jimmy: That's great, Mother! Call us in time to wash up for supper.

Mother: (*going out*) Almost ready now, children. I smell the muffins! (*to herself*) Well, they are not sick, that is sure. I guess they were just hungry!

Jimmy: Pretty nice Mother, isn't she, Susie?

Susie: Yes; and she certainly can make good muffins!
(*Dog barks and enters as before.*)

Jimmy: Come on, Towser, old fellow, good doggie—good doggie—up on the see-saw, old boy—up, up. He is better than an elephant, isn't he, Susie?
(*Dog on center of see-saw wags tail and then howls and jumps down. Exits, still howling.*)

Susie: But he is howling again, Jimmy. Do you think he hears the Fairy again?

Jimmy: Oh, I don't want any more trips, do you, Susie? What shall we say to her? Think of something, Susie —you always have good ideas.
(*Bugle blows.*)

Susie: I think it would be nice just to thank her politely.
(*Fairy appears, flies about and then stands on see-saw.*)

Fairy: Here you are home again. I'm sorry your trip was so short. Wouldn't you like to go back tomorrow?

Jimmy: Oh, thank you, *no,* Miss Fairy! You see we have to go to school and Sunday School—and another thing, our mother needs us around here.

Fairy: That is too bad. But you remember that I am a Wishing Fairy, Jimmy, and if I hear you wish for a change I'll come and get you. I know a giant—oh! twice as big as that one!

Jimmy: Thank you, Miss Fairy—but we think we'll stay here if you don't mind.

Fairy: All right—goodbye, children!

   (Fairy flies up and away.)

Susie: There! That was nice, Jimmy!

Jimmie: Thank you, Susie. Say, let's sing that see-saw song, Susie—I like to hear you sing.

Susie: All right, Jimmy.

   (They sing as curtain goes down.)

   See-saw Marjorie Daw, etc.

CURTAIN

The Enchanted Princess

A play for marionettes, in three scenes

Characters: The cat, the mean old woman, Mary, two
dwarfs, a woodchopper, three fairies, the King, his
Jester, the Prince and several tiny fairies.

There are three figures of Mary. In the first act her
expression is rather sad. She wears an apron over her dress.
For the second act she is made with a happier expression.
Flowers are in her hair. She has a dress exactly the same as
in the first act but no apron. In the third act she has a sweet,
rather dignified expression and a gown as beautiful as can
be made—pale yellow satin, lace and jewels are lovely.

There are two cats—one small and one large.

Two magic carpets are needed—one small and one large.
The large one is used in the second act with the large cat—
it gives the illusion that Mary has grown small while flying
through the air.

The small cat and carpet are used in the first and third
acts.

The woodchopper in the second act is so huge that only
his legs show. They are life size—real trousers and shoes.
A stick as high as the background is run through each
trouser leg and nailed to the back of the shoe. Fasten
the top of the trousers to the sticks so that you can grasp
each leg to swing it in a natural walk.

"THE JESTER"

Scene I. Home of the mean old woman. Paisley shawl background; brown material draped over wings; table and chair left of center back; small magic carpet close to back as possible at right of center; steps going up at right exit, if you like.

As curtain rises small cat is discovered on table lapping cream out of dish.

Old woman: (enters from right and stands at top of steps) Stizt! Stizt! You bad cat! Stop this minute! Turtle eggs and caterpillars! By the great horn spoon, you have lapped up all my cream! Get down from that table! Scat!

Cat: (jumps down and rests over by the left wing) Meow Meow.

Old woman: Hungry were you! Well, why don't you catch the mice? That is what you are here for—to catch the mice! A fine cat you are!

Cat: Meow! Meow!

Old woman: Be quiet! *(walks around looking at floor, table, steps)* Dust—I do believe! Where can that good-for-nothing Mary be? In the garden chasing butterflies I suppose! I enchanted a royal princess and brought her here to do my housework. Does she do it? Oh, no! The place hasn't been swept today. Ma-ry—Ma-ry—where is that girl? Ma-ry—Ma-ry!

Mary: (entering left) Yes, good mother.

Old woman: Come in, come in, don't stand there.

Mary: Yes, good mother. *(comes in and sits down in chair)*

Old woman: Get up, get up!　You lazy thing, where have you been?

Mary: In the garden.　*(rises)*

Old woman: You should stay in the house.　The cat stole my cream—it was your fault!

Mary: I'm sorry.

Old woman: Sorry doesn't bring the cream back!　Have you swept today?

Mary: Yes, good mother.

Old woman: Have you dusted?

Mary: Yes, good mother.

Old woman: Have you made the beds and washed the dishes?

Mary: Yes, good mother.

Old woman: Have you fed the hens and churned the butter?

Mary: Yes, good mother.

Old woman: Then you had better start the stew—brown the onions and the meat—cut the carrots fine, remember —give the tops to the cat—then let the stew simmer— don't let it boil hard—you hear me?　Don't let it boil hard!

Mary: Yes, good mother—*No,* good mother!

Old woman: (mimicking Mary) Yes, good mother—no, good mother.　Is that all you can say?　I'll go to town now.　Keep an eye on the cat.

(Old woman goes up steps and on out as she talks.)

Mary: (crosses stage slowly, pausing at table as she goes) What a mean old woman!　She is never happy and kind and she won't let anyone else be happy!　I try so hard to please her but she always scolds! *(She sits on steps and cries.)*

Cat: *(crosses to her, talking as he goes)* Don't cry, Mary —please don't cry!

Mary: *(lifts head in surprise)* What! You can talk?

Cat: Yes, I can talk because I am not really a cat.

Mary: Not a cat? You look like a cat!

Cat: I know I do, but I'm not. I was a prince and the old woman changed me into a cat because she had so many rats and mice! But, oh, Mary, how I hate rats and mice!

Mary: How dreadful! A prince changed into a cat!

Cat: Yes, Mary, I am a prince and you yourself are a princess. She enchanted you because she needed someone to do her housework for her.

Mary: Oh! I'm so glad I don't really belong to her—and I can almost remember my father the King! How sad he must be! If only we could get away from here, how wonderful it would be!

Cat: I know how to do it, Mary—I have been waiting for a chance to tell you. Last night when the old woman thought I was asleep under the table, she came in, rubbed her bony old hands, creaked her bony old knees and sat down on this little old carpet you sweep every day. Then she said some strange words and it flew away with her—right up and out of the window!

Mary: Oh! do you think we could do that? Would it carry us?

Cat: I thought we could try. You sit down first, Mary—

are you comfortable? Now I'll try the charm. *(sits on Mary's lap)* Ab-i-cum, ab-i-cum, zee-zoo-za!

Mary: It doesn't move. Are you sure that is right?

Cat: Perhaps it is zee-zoo-zum. Let's try it together.

Both: Ab-i-cum, ab-i-cum, zee-zoo-zum! Oh! it moves—it moves!

(Carpet slowly rises and floats back and forth across stage, up and off.)

CURTAIN

DWARF AND HIS BROTHER

Scene II. *Background—trees, sky and gold castle, with huge flowers at right and left front edge and vines and flowers on the wings. Dwarfs seated in center of stage, facing each other. Fairies hidden behind the front flowers.*

Curtain rises to music ("Dance of the Goblins" by Recker-Loraine.)
Dwarfs keep time with their hands, then jump up and do an eccentric dance, still keeping time with each other. As music reaches appropriate part the dwarfs run off right and the magic carpet slowly descends, floating back and forth across stage and settles to the ground at right of center, close against background. Large cat is used this time with Mary number two on large magic carpet.

Mary: Wake up, wake up! We have reached Fairyland!
(They get off the carpet.)

Cat: It was passing over that cat-nip field that made me so sleepy! Why how small you are, Mary!

Mary: Why so I am! You look huge. And my apron has blown away!

Cat: Oh, I'm so sleepy! I think I'll take a nap. *(He lies down at left center back.)*
(Dwarfs enter right.)

First brother: (to Mary and cat) Who are you? What are you doing here?

Mary: We are just visiting Fairyland. Do you live here?

First brother: Do we live here, brother?

Second brother: (deep voice and huge laugh) Ha-Ha-Ha —yes, we live here. We live in a tree.

Mary: Do you keep house?

First brother: Do we keep house, brother?

Second brother: Ha-Ha-Ha! Yes, we keep house.

Mary: Do you cook and wash dishes?

First brother: Do we cook and wash dishes, brother?

Second brother: Ha-Ha-Ha! No, we don't cook and wash dishes. We use leaves for dishes, we do.

First brother: Say, little girl, you'd better hide—the woodchopper's coming!

Mary: I'm not afraid of a woodchopper.

First brother: You would be if he stepped on you!
(Dwarfs exit right.)

Mary: Oh, mercy me—I forgot I'm so small! Yes, I'll hide, I'll hide!
(Whistle is heard, growing louder and louder. Mary exits left to hide. Woodchopper crosses stage from

*right to left, whistling. Mary enters left when whistle
has died away.)*

Mary: Oh, my! Are you all right, cat?

Cat: Yes—don't disturb me. This is the first good rest I've
had—*(jumps up)* Mary! Was that a mouse I heard?
*(Music off stage—"Venezia Waltz" by L. C. Desormes
—and fairy flies up from behind flowers at front of
stage.)*

Mary: No—it is a fairy—oh, what a lovely, lovely fairy!
*(runs toward her, but fairy always flies away. Mary
dances about the stage. More fairies appear from the
grass and flowers and the queen comes from above.)*

Mary: Oh, won't you come with me, or let me stay with
you?

(Fairies disappear upward as lights dim slowly.)

Cat: It is getting late, Mary, we ought to go.

Mary: Yes, it is getting dark. Where shall we go? I don't
like to think of going back to the mean old woman—she
would be so angry with us! What do *you* think?

Cat: How would it be to try to reach your father's palace?

Mary: Oh, we could try! Come, hurry before it is dark!
(They sit on the carpet, the cat getting on last.)

Cat: Are you ready?

Mary: Yes—let us say the charm.

Both: Ab-i-cum, ab-i-cum, zee-zoo-zum!
(They float upwards and off.)

Mary: *(as they disappear)* We are moving! We are moving! Hold tight!

CURTAIN

"THE ENCHANTED PRINCESS"

Scene III. Tapestry background, velvet hangings on the wings, rose spotlight. King seated on the throne, slightly left of center back. Prince is hidden behind the throne.

(Curtain rises to music—"The Boy and the Birds" by Fred W. Hager—as Jester dances in from left.)

Jester: Oh, Your Majesty, *do* cheer up. I'm sure they'll find your daughter!

King: No, I'm afraid there is magic connected with her disappearance! I'll never see her again!

Jester: Have patience a little longer, O King. See, I'll dance for you. *(capers about)* Oh, I know a riddle— Ha-Ha-Ha! I haven't got it, I don't want it, but if I had it I wouldn't take the world for it!

King: Ah—that is old. I know the answer—a bald head!

Jester: (very much pleased) Yes, yes, you are right, it is a bald head! I know another—

> As I was going to St. Ives,
> I met a man with seven wives,
> Each wife had seven sacks
> Each sack had seven cats
> Each cat had seven kits—
> Kits, cats, sacks and wives
> How many were going to St. Ives?

King: Oh, be still! Go help find my little daughter!

Jester: (weeping) Woe is me—woe is me! I am no longer the funny man I used to be! *(exits still weeping.)*

King: *(bowing his head)* Oh, my little daughter, where are you, where are you?

(The small carpet floats down—to music, if you like—with Mary in a beautiful gown and the small cat used in the first act on her lap. It settles slowly down at right of center back, and they get off.)

Cat: Here we are, little Princess! Oh, see how your dress has changed! *(He goes across to the left of the King. Mary remains standing at the right.)*

Mary: Oh, there is my father! See how sad he seems! Father, Father! *(goes to his side.)*

King: *(astonished, he puts his arm around the Princess)* Oh, my little daughter! How glad I am to have you home again! How did you come?

Mary: The black cat brought me on the magic carpet!

King: Black cat! Magic carpet!

Mary: You see, Father, I was enchanted by a mean old woman. I had to keep house for her—sweep, cook and wash!

King: We must reward the cat— Ah! we have the very thing! O Foolish Fool, bring me the correct present for this cat. You had one this morning.

Jester: *(entering left)* Welcome Little Princess, Welcome! *(he holds out two rats hanging by tails tied together)* There, Your Majesty, two of them!

Mary: Oh, no! Take them away. Take them away! He hates them!

Jester: I go—I go! *(exits left)*

King: What do you mean, daughter?

Mary: Why he really isn't a cat at all—he is a Prince. He was enchanted by the old woman, too, and it was he who saw the old woman use the magic carpet. We went to Fairyland and then here! Oh, can't you think of something splendid for him, Father?

King: Let me think—Yes, I have it! Little cat you shall be rewarded. Listen carefully— This throne upon which I sit is a magic throne. He who goes seven times around the throne and wishes as he goes, shall have his wish! So seven times round, little cat, and wish as you go!

(Music—"Pomp and Circumstance March," by Elgar. Cat goes around six times and then the seventh time he stays hidden behind the throne and the Prince comes forth. Listen carefully and you will find that the music changes at just the right time.)

Mary: Oh, Father, Father, how wonderful, how wonderful!

Prince: (*kneeling—if he won't kneel beautifully, though he should, have him bow instead*) Oh, Your Majesty, I thank you with all my heart. At last I am once more a man.

King: And you shall have my daughter for your bride, for I can see that you love each other.

(The Prince crosses over toward Mary as the magic carpet flies away.)

Mary: (*waving handkerchief*) Goodbye, Magic Carpet, Goodbye! (*fairies appear*) Oh, the fairies have come! (*The King rises as flowers flutter down.*)

King: A blessing on you, dear children, and happiness for ever and ever.

(The Prince and Mary start toward each other, bowing toward audience and each other.)

CURTAIN

The Tragic Tale of Pierrot
A Pantomime in three scenes

Characters: Columbine, Pierrot, Harlequin and the dog.

Music: Gay minuet music is suitable for Columbine's dance and more dramatic music should be selected for Harlequin—minor music is good. Parts of "I Pagliacci" and "The Funeral March of a Marionette" make a splendid finale. Piano or violin is better than a phonograph for pantomime as the music can be continuous throughout.

Scene I.—Setting: Any fantastic back-drop.
Columbine is discovered dancing. Pierrot enters, is overwhelmed by the beauty of Columbine. He woos and wins her.

Scene II.—Setting: Outdoor back-drop showing a picturesque house out of which Columbine, Pierrot and the dog have, presumably, just come. Columbine carries her market basket, the handle hooked over her hand. The lovers reluctantly bid each other farewell, Pierrot turning back again and again but finally exits right, still waving. The dog follows.
Columbine remains gazing after Pierrot. Harlequin enters left. Fascinated by Columbine he approaches, expressing his mad infatuation with eloquent gestures. Col-

111

umbine repels his advances at first but finally overcome by his passionate overtures flees with him, dropping her basket as she goes.   They exit left.

Scene III.—Setting: Same as Scene II.

Dog enters right, sniffs at the basket, runs excitedly about looking for Columbine.

Pierrot enters right.   The dog rushes from him to the basket and back again, then exits left.

Pierrot, alarmed, examines the basket, then turns to the house.   He peers through the window—the house is empty —Columbine has forsaken him!

Overcome by grief, Pierrot, his head drooping, steps slowly forward and raising his hands to heaven, falls to the ground, broken-hearted!

CURTAIN

An Oriental Sketch

(Arranged for the delectation of "grown-ups")

Cast: The Old Amir, the Favorite, the Black Boy, the Wicked One (rival of the Favorite), the small poisonous snake.

A suitable background is a small silk or velvet rug.

Music for "The Favorite" is easy to find—here is a list of suggestions:

"Danse Arabe" ....*Tschaikowsky*
"In a Persian Market" ....*Ketelbey*
"The Desert Wail" ....*Maloof*
"Romance" ....*Tschaikowsky*
For the Black Boy:—
"Danse Chinoise" ....*Tschaikowsky*
"Danse des Mirlitons" ....*Tschaikowsky*

For the Wicked One:—

"Kurdistan" ....*Maloof*

"Song of India Fox Trot"........*Adapted from Rimsky-*
Korsakov's "Chanson Indoue"

The Curtain rises.

The Old Amir is sitting on a cushion. The Favorite is reclining on a luxurious couch, gently waving a soft black feather fan to the rhythm of the Oriental music. She languidly rises, moves with undulating motion toward the Old Amir. She poses before him. Slowly swaying and bending to the music, she kneels and bows to the floor before the Amir. With his hand he waves her away. Slowly she returns to the couch and casts herself upon it.

At a sign from the Old Amir the Black Boy enters (to his music) carrying a basket tray of flowers. He skips about, kneels before the Amir, then approaches the Favorite. He showers her with his flowers and exits still dancing.

The Wicked One now enters, dancing seductively. (Use only one-half the record.) Her green chiffon veil sweeps the floor behind her; held in her two hands it gives added fascination to her dance.

The Amir is enraptured by her vivaciousness. He nods his head with delight. Off she dances with many backward glances.

At a signal from the Amir the Black Boy enters (to his music), kneels before the Amir, and at his gestured command lowers his tray to the floor. The small, very dangerous snake wriggles into the tray. The Black Boy dances with it—the snake darting its head to right and left. He lowers the tray in front of the erstwhile Favorite—the serpent slithers to the floor—glides up over the prostrate Favorite, who is paralyzed with horror (as is also the audience). With a rapid dart it poisons her—she is dead!

The Black Boy stands horrified at the head of the couch.

The Wicked One enters (to her music) and pauses in her dance to glance with satisfaction at the poisoned Favorite. Triumphantly she dances until she falls exhausted at the feet of the Amir.

CURTAIN